AF226136

Beyond the
MARRIAGE Bed

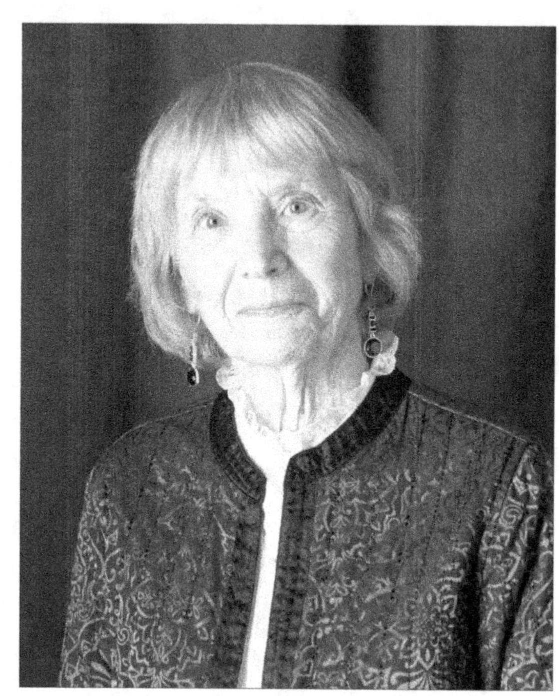

HELEN MURRAY SIPALA

Beyond the MARRIAGE Bed

My Years as Friend, Model and Confidante of Andrew Wyeth

By Helen Murray Sipala

Edited by Bruce E. Mowday and Simsun Greco

REGENT PRESS
Berkeley, California
2021

Beyond the MARRIAGE Bed
Copyright © 2021 by Helen Sipala
All rights reserved

ISBN 13: 978-1-58790-559-9

ISBN 10: 1-58790-559-0

Library of Congress Cataloging-in-Publication Data

Names: Sipala, Helen Murray, author. | Mowday, Bruce E., editor.
Title: Beyond The marriage bed : my years as friend, model and confidante
 of Andrew Wyeth / by Helen Murray Sipala ; edited by Bruce E. Mowday and
 Simsun Greco.
Other titles: Diaries. Selections
Description: Berkeley, California : Regent Press, 2021. | Summary:
Identifiers: LCCN 2021001216 | ISBN 9781587905599 (hardback)
Subjects: LCSH: Sipala, Helen Murray--Diaries. | Artists' models--United
 States--Diaries. | Sipala, George E., 1929-2020. | Wyeth, Andrew,
 1917-2009--Friends and associates--Diaries.
Classification: LCC N7574.4 .S57 2021 | DDC 702.8--dc23
LC record available at https://lccn.loc.gov/2021001216

For information, address Helen Sipala
1421 Baltimore Pike
Chadds Ford, PA 19317

Cover photograph taken by George Sipala
as Andrew Wyeth was making a study for his painting The Marriage Bed.

Printed in the United States of America
REGENT PRESS
Berkeley, California
www.regentpress.net

Dedication

To Andy:

Yes Andy, I did write it down just as you "hoped" I would. I think you would
be proud that the world now knows the REAL Andy: sensitive, generous,
compassionate, comical, humble and a true gentleman!

Contents

Dedication ... 5

Foreword ... 9

Editor's Note ... 11

Acknowledgments ... 12

Introduction ... 13

A Condolence Letter to Betsy Wyeth ... 15

Chapter One 1989: *Meeting Andy* ... 17

Chapter Two 1990: *World Premiere* ... 32

Chapter Three 1991: *Andy Shares His Soul* ... 46

Chapter Four 1992: *Andy Is on Cloud Nine* ... 70

Chapter Five 1993: *N. C. Wyeth Was an Excellent Critic* ... 83

Chapter Six 1994: *Life's Fragilities* ... 120

Chapter Seven 1995: *Shocking Element* ... 126

Chapter Eight 1996: *Different Type of Perspective* ... 131

Chapter Nine 1997: *Andy Receives a "Rousing Welcome"* ... 137

Chapter Ten 1998: *Andy Enchants Phyllis Diller* ... 141

Chapter Eleven 1999: *Andy Paints Victoria* ... 148

Chapter Twelve 2000: *Last Conversation With N. C. Wyeth* ... 154

Chapter Thirteen 2001: *Andy Suffers a Serious Pneumonia Attack* ... 161

Chapter Fourteen 2002: *Helga Room of Nudes* ... 161

Chapter Fifteen 2003: *She Keeps Me Alive* ... 174

Chapter Sixteen 2004: *Betsy Was Right for Andy and His Work* ... 179

Chapter Seventeen 2005: *God Help Our Wonderful Friend* ... 184

Chapter Eighteen 2006: *Like Making Love in Public* ... 189

Chapter Nineteen 2007: *A Presidential Tour of the White House* ... 193

Chapter Twenty 2008: *I Love You* ... 196

Chapter Twenty-One 2009: *May God Bless Andy Wherever He Is* ... 198

Postscript: *Correspondence* ... 202

Editor-In-Chief ... 206

Foreword

When Helen Sipala first approached me about the Beyond the Marriage Bed book project, I was fascinated. The subject was intriguing. Not often does a writer get a chance to delve into the relationship of a famed artist, in this case Andrew Wyeth, and his confidante and model, Helen. Before agreeing to take part in this venture, I wanted to know more about the diary and Helen's goals for the book. After my first reading of Helen's whole diary, which includes hundreds of type-written pages, letters and drawings made by Andrew, I knew the subject was unique and special. I didn't realize how special the chronicle was until reviewing the diary a second and third time while determining which passages would be included in Beyond the Marriage Bed and the structure of this book.

Helen said she wanted this book to portray Andrew Wyeth as the man she saw in her eyes. She told me "don't sugar coat it." Andrew wanted a spot-on rendering of him as an artist and a person. Andrew didn't come right out and ask Helen to record their many meetings during almost two decades. He did mention several times that he hoped Helen was taking notes; a clear indication Andrew was a silent and willing partner in this work.

Helen has achieved her goal of fleshing out Andrew Wyeth. She had almost daily interactions with Andrew during a period of about two decades. She was faithful in recording her thoughts and observations. She not only defines her image of Andrew but also reveals the way Andrew Wyeth, the artist, worked in the final decades of his life. The relationship Andrew had with his models is fascinating. And, Helen reveals a lot about herself and her character in the passages.

Helen considers herself a close friend and confidante of Andrew. The pair had many intimate discussions about life, religion and the family and friends in Andrew's life. Helen's home, Painter's Folly, became not only an inspiration for Andrew's work but also a safe haven for the artist. Beyond the Marriage Bed is not a fawning look at Andrew Wyeth through the eyes of a star-struck fan or model, even though Helen believes Andrew was a master talent and great artist. At times Helen questions Andrew's motivations and actions. She certainly didn't believe everything Andrew said. She isn't fond of many of Andrew's habits. This book doesn't "sugar coat" elements of Andrew's life.

The book is written in a spirit of honesty and love. Helen's intention wasn't to attack or demean anyone in Andrew's world. Helen has achieved that goal but she doesn't "sugar coat" troubling incidents in Andrew's life and their relationship. She is transparent about her thoughts and her relationship with Andrew and George, her husband.

— Bruce E. Mowday
MAY 2020

Editor's Note

An explanation is needed as to the structure of this book. All of the entries in italics are taken from Helen's diary. Because of the length of some of the entries, the text has been lightly edited in certain passages. We've taken great care to condense the diary, as it runs many hundreds of pages, without altering the message. The passages deleted, we believe, are either redundant or failed to advance the story of the relationship between Helen and George and Andrew. Bridge passages have been added between diary entries to give readers a background as to people and places mentioned and to summarize circumstances and exchanges.

To be sure, this is Helen's story of Andrew Wyeth. She has reviewed the manuscript and has approved the final text.

Beyond the Marriage Bed is an intimate look at Andrew Wyeth the artist and the man and his close relationship with Helen Sipala, model and confidante. We hope readers enjoy this rare glimpse into the world of a true and talented artist through Helen's 20-year diary.

Acknowledgments

I've received support from many friends and family members during the writing and publishing of this book. I appreciate the faith they placed in me and their persistent encouragement.

Robert S. Porter is recognized for his expert photography contributions. Susan S. Drumheller aided with the research and her effort is greatly appreciated.

My good friends Rob and Robin Newman provided a solution for every problem encountered and gave a much needed push to move forward with this project.

The final wish of George, my late husband, was for this book to be completed. His desire has been fulfilled.

Introduction

Andrew Wyeth had visited our home for about a week when someone suggested that I keep a diary. I really was not excited to do so as I thought his visits would be few and far between.

Over the years, he stated several times that he hoped I "was writing all this down." You will see by my notes when this happened I never responded to him. It was a known fact Andy preferred that writers not make his stories "sweet" but to "put an edge to it."

I reviewed my notes and deleted the most harmful statements, even though they were true. Andy was blunt and it is human nature for people to misbehave, speak out of turn, vie for attention and sometimes create havoc. George and I are included in this group. It would be impossible for George and me to be perfect on a daily basis for 20+ years. We were naïve in so many ways.

I think our secret to a wonderful relationship with Andy was humor! From day one we treated him as a friend, not as a celebrity or star. I know he would agree that we were loyal, protective, cordial and goofy. He made a match with us. He loved my local country background and the history of our circa 1856 home Painter's Folly, which included Howard Pyle, N. C. Wyeth and Andy as a child.

George and I made a point of not intruding into the personal life of Andy and Betsy. We never called or visited without invitation and we never asked for anything. We knew our place in their social circles. Without Andy we would never fit in but because of Andy we were always welcomed at parties and special events. Andy purposely made this happen.

I remind people that Andy came into our lives, not us into his. We moved to Chadds Ford because of the house, not much aware of the Wyeth family and their close proximity. Little did we know that Andy was eager and delighted to find a hiding place and a home away from his home. The timing was perfect for our relationship.

During our morning teas, Andy had a tendency to over-exaggerate or dramatize facts for shock or entertainment. Theatrics was a big part of him, beginning as a child. Also, he led a very private and secret life for many reasons. As a result, some of the information Andy told me might not be real or correct. When I confronted Andy with my doubts, he would say, "Well, if it isn't true it oughta be." As you can see by my diary notes, those interactions were frustrating at times.

Andy was extremely loyal to us, as he was to all his true friends. When we made mistakes before his family and friends, Andy was the first person to defend us. If we truly had a problem, he would scout around for influential help to aid us, such as when PennDOT wanted to take some of our property for road expansion. If anyone insulted us regarding our posing for his paintings, he would seek revenge upon the offending person. If he felt our house could use a facelift in any way, he made it happen. Those improvements enhanced the very painting he was creating at the time. His efforts to preserve this historical property would make him proud as he believed Painter's Folly belonged to the art world.

Helen Sipala
May 2020

A Condolence Letter to Betsy Wyeth

(This letter was written by Helen Sipala at the time of Andy's death.)

January 20, 2009

Dear Betsy and Family,

We are thinking of you during this very difficult time. We send our love, thoughts and prayers. George and I have also lost a dear and loyal friend in Andy.

Twenty years ago he entered our lives and never left. It started with tea in the kitchen on an almost daily basis. He brought friends, relatives and the notables to join us. We became friends with all his friends and learned so much from them.

He was quick to send invitations our way, shared jokes, stories, memories and, oh, how the laughter filled the kitchen! I can still hear him ask, "What's new?" as he poured too much sugar in his tea. No matter what I served he thought it delicious and, as a true gentleman, never turned it down.

For years he knew where the key was but we removed it when the house was being repaired. After that we got up at six o'clock every morning, turned lights on, unlocked the door and went back to bed in case he came because he was an early bird. He loved to sneak in and surprise us in bed.

We played jokes on Andy with hide and seek, costumes, scary masks, wigs and silly toys. We were comfortable with doing this within the first few months of our friendship and he started reciprocating in the same devilish way.

I remember when he asked me to pose I looked in the mirror and was puzzled as to why. Was I homely, ultra-country or unusual? I knew I wasn't handicapped or voluptuous. Art was a mystery. How naïve I was!

He seldom came empty handed. It might be sharing a canned good, a leftover breakfast muffin, a book, and an unwanted piece of mail or a joke. If he gave us anything significant I would protest and he would always say, "But why not, you're my friends." That's very humbling.

If we goofed, he forgave us, if we faltered, he directed us. He simplified our view on life but elevated us. He changed us in many ways. I conveyed these sentiments to him many, many times, especially before he went to Maine every year. I never took him for granted. So many memories, so much joy and a real honor to know him.

We will miss him dearly, especially at Christmas. This past Christmas he stopped in during the morning and had his last cup of tea with us. It was touching.

Thank you for accepting us as Andy's friends with such love and inclusion.

Love,
Helen Sipala

*March 8, 1992: An emotional conversation for both of us. He is a very
compassionate man and I asked him how many people know the REAL ANDY.
He responded, 'None.' How sad. He is easily moved to tears
and I respect him for that.*

CHAPTER ONE
1989

Meeting Andy

The first snow storm of the winter of 1989 in Chadds Ford, Pennsylvania, took place on March 1, St. David's Day. Helen and George Sipala were in their home, Painter's Folly, the house built in 1857 by Samuel Painter and once owned by famed artist Howard Pyle. Pyle used the house as the base for the more than 200 students he taught, including N. C. Wyeth. Pyle and his students began what is recognized as the Brandywine School of Art.

> *March 1, 1989: I saw a man with a parka hood at the bank by the
> pool. The head was bobbing up and down. I told George to
> check him out. George could see a man painting the house and
> ignored him.*
> *March 2: Same man sketching the house in same position by the pool.
> Paid no attention.*

The next day, as George retrieved a newspaper, the same man approached George and asked if he could paint the house. George recognized Andrew Wyeth. "Oh! You know me?" was Andy's response. George and Andy talked about Andy's father, N. C. Wyeth, and N. C. painting in the house with Pyle. George invited Andy to return and tour Painter's Folly.

The brief encounter was the beginning of a new, wonderful and exciting segment of life for George and Helen.

> *March 5: George and I returned from church about 9:30 a.m. and*
> *passed Andy leaving our driveway. We waited in the parking lot*
> *in case he returned. He did. I was introduced. We teased him*
> *about his bobbing head at the pool. He paid me a compliment,*
> *saying to George: "You have an attractive wife." He then left.*

Helen offered to give Andy a tour of Painter's Folly and Andy quickly accepted the invitation.

> *March 8: Andy arrives dressed in an ankle length Coyote fur coat,*
> *polyester jacket, turtleneck white shirt, trousers a little short*
> *and boot shoes. We tour the house, pour over pictures and*
> *memorabilia in the family room. All the while, we are taking*
> *pictures and movies (which didn't turn out because we were*
> *too excited). Poor Andy's nose ran from the cold house and his*
> *sinus problems. We had our book "Wyeth at Kuerners" out and*
> *brought it to his attention. He asked, "Would you like me to*
> *sign it?" Then he did. We had muffins and coffee and sent a bag*
> *of muffins home with him.*

For the next few weeks, Andy stopped to sketch and paint. He stayed for coffee and had a look at the widow's walk section of Painter's Folly. Later, widow's walk would become a favorite place for Andy to paint. Helen invited Andy and his wife Betsy for Sunday tea.

> *April 9: Tea – chicken salad miniature fancy sandwiches, apricot*
> *bars, strawberries in chocolate basket, minted ladyfingers w/*
> *cream, sliced plum cake. Ate in the living room. She was dressed*
> *in a safari outfit complete with hat. Came in kitchen door,*
> *warm reception. Andy always gives me a big hug and kiss (warm*
> *person). We give complete tour. Good time!*

Andy and Betsy reciprocated by inviting Helen and George to their nearby home, the Mill, and the Brandywine River Museum of Art, the museum which showcases the works of the Wyeth family of artists.

> *April 27: George and I went to the Wyeth's home. Andy took us for a*
> *"cook's tour" while Betsy prepared fried corkscrew hor'd'oeuvres*
> *(fried pasta looking things). We took a basket with a napkin,*
> *bottle of champagne and four glasses for a toast. They invited us*
> *to the museum the next day for a private tour.*
>
> *April 28: At the museum we were to ask for "Mrs. Andrew Wyeth in*
> *the Oval office." She came down and embraced us both and took*
> *us upstairs. We saw the vault of paintings, her jewelry collection,*
> *belt collection, cataloging project, "Bones" (or Self Portrait) and*
> *she ended the tour with us in the Wyeth's gallery and "Snow*
> *Hill." She showed us sketches never shown before and Andy's*
> *first signed painting (a boat). She embraces us both again in*
> *goodbye.*

During the following five weeks, Andy spent 11 days painting in the widow's walk and visiting Helen and George. The couple shared breakfast of fruit and pastries with Andy. Andy painted even when the couple wasn't home. Andy was given free access to Painter's Folly. On June 2, George left a note: "Food in refig." Andy took the food and George's note and left a sketch for Helen and George. The close relationship between Andy and the couple was forming.

> *June 11: Andy gave slippers to George and a photo of our house*
> *to me. Nicky Wyeth arrived from N. Y. to visit his father*
> *and stopped in here. Stayed for a breakfast of pancakes with*
> *blueberries, mangos (the first for Andy), cantaloupe, honeydew,*
> *egg coddlers (first for both of them), apricot juice and coffee. We*
> *walked to the (Brandywine) battlefield and toured the cemetery.*
> *Nicky then toured our house and yard and departed. Andy*
> *surveyed the outside of our house and yard for different angles to*
> *paint.*

Andy's youth was spent amidst the fantasies his father N. C. Wyeth created for his book illustrations. Robin Hood was one of his favorites. The love of costumes and imaginary worlds held a fascination for Andy for his whole life. Helen and George were invited to enter Andy's fantasies. At times, George dressed in characters from Wyeth paintings.

> *June 12: Andy was here and went to the red maple tree. George
> dressed in a boob costume, German helmet, and Andy's black
> slippers. He showed Andy the "parts" of Kuerner, Helga & Andy.
> Good laugh!*

Later the same day Andy returned with one of his models, Helga Testorf. Andy did a series of more than 240 paintings and drawings of Helga, many of them nude, between 1971 and 1985. The paintings were done in secret as neither Andy's wife Betsy nor Helga's husband John knew of the paintings. The paintings were stored at Big Bend, the home of George "Frolic" Weymouth, Andy's good friend and benefactor of the Brandywine River Museum and Conservancy.

Helga was born in Germany and spent time in a Prussian Protestant convent before becoming ill and departing. She studied to be a nurse and a masseuse before coming to the United States with her husband where they raised their family of four children. She also cared for Andy's neighbor Karl Kuerner Sr. Kuerner was a model for Andy and was depicted in his World War I German uniform.

A sensation in the art world took place in 1986 when the existence of the Helga paintings became public. The Helga series was featured in news articles across the world. Philadelphia publisher and millionaire Leonard E. B. Andrews purchased almost the entire series. Later, the paintings were sold to a Japanese company for an estimated $40 million.

> *June 12: Andy and Helga arrived in separate cars. She goes in the
> house with Andy, walking throughout. George called me at my
> office and I arrive while Helga is upstairs. I meet Helga on the
> 3rd floor while softly calling her name. Helga drops her head
> and picks up the pace, walking past me and out of the house.
> An offer of tea or coffee is ignored and Andy can't talk her
> into staying. She says nothing. She is layered in several dresses,
> insulated vest, wrapped legs, sunglasses and hair in braids.
> The temperature was about 80 degrees. She gets in her car and
> leaves.
> Andy stays a while and starts to sketch me for the first time on the
> 3rd floor in Richard's room (a son's bedroom) on the edge of a bed*

*by the window. Fascinated with my flared nostrils, high cheek bones,
devilish eyes and color tone. His motions are very animated and
talking is intermittent.*

Three days later Andy asked Helen and George to have dinner with
Howard and DeeDee Brokow. Howard was a nephew of artist Howard Pyle.
Brokow had never seen Painter's Folly.

*June 16: Andy comes dressed in a Nehru shirt, sport coat and
wader's pants that were at least three inches too short. They
brought Howard Pyle's genealogy book. We showed them the
house. George took pictures. Howard was intent on reminiscing
with his long-time friend, Andy. At the Dilworthtown Inn, we
met Dr. Joseph Valloti. (Andy & Betsy's personal physician.) A
short fellow, 65 yrs. of age & very pleasant. Howard dominated
the conversation. I felt sorry for Joe. Hopefully, he appreciated
my attention while sitting next to him. There was no sign of
the check. The staff knew Andy and treated him royally. It was
Andy's treat.*

The evening of the Dilworthtown Inn dinner Helen and George gave Andy
a birthday gift of a drawing by Frank Sipala, George's brother, with the nota-
tion: "May you experience the same deep joy that we have enjoyed in sharing
our home with you – July 12, 1989 – Love, Helen & George."
Helen noted observations in her diary:

*Andy has a great sense of humor, tells jokes (tastefully off-color),
does great impersonations, and has an infectious laughter.
Andy has an unusual figure: chest bone protrudes with very slim
arms, very slim waist with only a slight ripple of fold about the
hips, very thin legs, 10 1/2 narrow foot (they look oversized next
to his skinny body). His hands have long fingers with signs of
arthritis – twisting a few.
He brushes his gray/blond hair forward giving a full affect with
lots of waves. His blue eyes have drooping lids. He is tan, with
character wrinkles and capped teeth.*

> *Andy is genuinely warm, most humble, generous, mannerly, most*
> *appreciative, a real gentleman. He is affectionate and shows it*
> *with family and us. He was all of this from the first day of our*
> *meeting.*
> *He has trouble remembering the pronunciation of Sipala and*
> *says it twice most of the time.*
> *Andy is nicely casual when eating and uses fingers many times.*
> *He always offers to do the dishes. He notices any and all effort*
> *put into serving food and was taught to eat everything presented.*
> *His meals are usually fish or fowl, likes fruit and drinks black*
> *coffee.*
> *We think our jokes and laughter make Andy comfortable, he is*
> *entertained as a close friend.*
> *The excitement has increased since March. We have trouble*
> *sleeping and rehash events over and over, thinking of small*
> *remarks dropped with special meaning and excitement. In the*
> *beginning we shared small details with our friends but avoided*
> *any real confidential information.*

Andy felt comfortable with Helen and George and invited friends, including Dee Parker, to the Sipala home. Parker, a Wyeth neighbor and model, was an art teacher. The couple assured Andy that they welcome his friends, including Helga.

> *June 19: Helga arrives at 8:30. Andy is in the widow's walk. She gets*
> *out of her car, gets in Andy's car, back in her car and drives off.*
> *She returns in about 10 minutes, gets out of her car and walks*
> *directly to our house. She opened the kitchen door and asks if*
> *Andy was here. We said, 'Yes, go on up. Do you know the way?'*
> *She didn't answer and walked upstairs. … Helga hesitated …*
> *then (exited) out the door. George tries to snap a picture of her*
> *through the door but is most fearful of her catching us. That*
> *would end it all with her. George sets a table for Andy as a joke*
> *with plates for Andy, George, Betsy, Helga, Seri, Dee, Helen*
> *and an Unknown Virgin. His note says, 'Andy's Harem by Chef*
> *George of the Manor.' Andy comes downstairs and howls with*

laughter. He enjoys the morning's events and lingers. He said
he painted Parker nude in Maine without Betsy's awareness.
He sold the painting, hoping it would be unnoticed. Phyllis
Wyeth (Andy's daughter-in-law and Jamie's wife) saw it in a
Washington mansion. President Bush asked if it was Helga.
Andy feels all hell will break loose if and when Betsy finds out!

Just a few months after Andy entered their lives, Helen and George's world had drastically changed.

June 20: Life is so exciting! Every day is like a Broadway show.
George and I laugh and literally squeal with the un-realness
of it all. Sex has become shelved and replaced with different
physical satisfactions and climaxes – a high that doesn't subside.
Andy has changed our lives in ways that he isn't aware. Every
kind gesture on our part is rewarded twofold by Andy – a totally
unselfish person. His stories are fascinating, lending a glimpse
into the world of the famous.

Helen and George were careful about sharing information about Andy with their friends. One friend was offended because a local restaurant wouldn't offer him the same special courtesies offered to Andy. The friend intended to berate the restaurant owners and the Sipalas were "mortified."

Andy's relationship had drastically changed the Sipalas' lives. The couple planned to sell Painter's Folly and use the proceeds as their retirement funds. They decided against doing so because Andy was using their home to paint. "I believe God will reveal his plans while we take each day at a time. Funds are tight, more than I like to reveal," Helen wrote.

June 21: Andy is in the widow's walk. He dropped off the book
about Helga. After I returned home I walked up to the roof and
climbed out to give him a hug and kiss of thanks. His shirt was
off and he was nicely tanned as he sat on a large paint bucket by
the roof chimney.
June 22: Andy talked of Helga's book and paintings. Mr. Testorf
(Helga's husband) told Andy not to paint her nude; Andy had

already done so and just continued to "walk through the hot water." Mr. Testorf has not spoken to him since. Betsy kept three of the Helga paintings. Leonard Andrews, who purchased the paintings, is preparing to sue for those three. Andy expects litigation. Brandywine River Museum is trying to raise funds for the collection but Andy doesn't think they can do so.

Betsy told Andy he must have found 'another woman' to paint (me) and Andy agreed. Hopefully Andy has lots of plans for me. It's exciting!

He told Helga she couldn't just walk into our house without speaking. He said, 'They are my friends.' Helga is fascinated with my hair, Andy said. I wear it short in back, ears cut out and permed on top. Evidently, she speaks of us when away. Interesting that she even noticed, as her eyes never meet ours.

George received a new camera for Father's Day and attempted to record life with Andy. George was nervous and his heart pounded with excitement as he ran around the house. Dr. Valloti sent the couple flowers for an upcoming dinner and George took photos. Helen recorded, "We are thrilled!"

June 25: Andy has coffee with us and we have lots of laughs. We talked about the du Pont family and how close knit they are. Phyllis Wyeth is the daughter of Felix du Pont. Jamie refused the spouse's share of the du Pont inheritance to preserve his independence when he married Phyllis.

Betsy is planning on doing something for us when she returns from Maine in appreciation for our hospitality to Andy. A good feeling! They call each other regularly, very unselfish and generous people. Andy will try to get Helga to join us tonight for dinner. I saw it as impossible. She does like Joe V.(Valloti) and he will be there.

Andy and Joe arrive at 6:30 p.m. Joe brings a bottle of wine and we have a drink before eating in the dining room. Crab appetizer, scallops, chicken fillets, string beans, carrots, strawberries with raspberry sauce and pound cake. We all had Vodka and tonic before dinner, Andy's favorite. Elegant and delicious! Andy is proud of our hospitality and most grateful.

Andy spent the next few months in Maine and didn't return to paint in the widow's walk until October.

*October 9: Great reunion! We had coffee, fruit and muffins. We
discussed painting me and possibly George (maybe together
looking through a window). We had a good laugh with the
posing possibilities. I think he is heading to a nude idea again.
Betsy thought it would be a good idea. Betsy is still in Maine
and she's angry because Andy left early.
Andy went to the widow's walk and froze while on the roof. He
came down and we had more coffee. He mentioned that Leonard
Andrews and Walter Annenberg could be fierce competitors.
Each had bought Andy's collections for high figures.*

*October 14: Andy was in the yard and he drove around to the pool
area and sat on top of it for a better view of the side of the
house. He ran into my flower garden and over the leg of the
end table. The sun was out for a short time and then it turned
gray. We sat on the porch and had coffee and melon and Andy
brought four muffins.*

*October 15: Andy and Joe Valloti came for dinner. Barbara Walters
(television news personality) was coming Monday (the next day)
and she wants Andy to do her painting. He doesn't want to do so
because Jamie already did it. He doesn't want to be interviewed
by her since all reporters now ask the big question about his
relationship with Helga. "Did you?'
Rudolf Nureyev is performing in the area and Andy might be
entertaining him at Phyllis's request. (Jamie did a series of
paintings of Nureyev.)Andy might bring Nureyev here. Who
knows???
Helen Valloti and Betsy are coming home from Maine
tomorrow.*

*October 25: He said he was going to bring Nureyev here last Sunday
but Rudolph was sick. We sat on the side porch. Andy told
George that his famous painting of Olson (background of golden*

*grass) was done with gold leaf. He never revealed this to anyone
else before in his life! (A painting secret.) Andrews sold the Olson
and Helga series to a national overseas syndicate. Smart move
for Andrews.*

*October 26: I went to work and missed Andy! Andy brought a basket
of flowers and 25 miniature pumpkins for me and left a note
"Happy Halloween." Andy painted in the side yard. We took
pictures from secret angles, hoping he wouldn't catch us. Oh! To
watch the master!!*

*October 29: Andy came with Nureyev. George and I were visiting the
kids. Andy took Nureyev through the house. He left us a note
with a drawing of a dancer. We were just sick, SICK! A thrill
just passed us by!*

Halloween was a special time for Andy. On October 31, Andy visited
dressed as a German general with Howard Pyle's long leather boots. He knocked
at the Sipalas' side door and had a nylon stocking over his face and a mask. The
uniform was from a dead German soldier and still had blood on it. He then
invited George and Helen to Jamie's house.

*October 31: I put on a shirt with sparkling lights, wig and mask.
George had on his aerobic outfit (he had taught that night) and
a mask. Costumed people lined the walkway to Jamie's house.
Some were lying on the ground and others sitting in the bushes
and on the porch. Scared us half to death! Jamie had a black
outfit with a pig mask. Phyllis was a snake charmer. Frolic
was exceptionally warm, kissed George and me and mentioned
getting together. He acted like we were old friends even though
we were only introduced once.*

Helen's modeling career began in earnest the day after Halloween.

*November 1: I'm to meet Andy at noon if sunny. George was working
and I was to pose. I stood inside my bedroom window and Andy
was outside on the roof. He asked me to bare my shoulders.
I took off my blouse, slip and bra and left my panty hose on,*

wrapped myself in a towel. Andy yelled to just "drop the towel."
I felt like Route 1 was an audience. I was more embarrassed
with the traffic than by Andy. I simply had to pretend Andy was
a physician, grit my teeth and 'bare' it. What could he see in the
55 yr. old woman!? Were the stories true about him and Helga?
Was I to be exploited? If so, I felt I had as much to gain as Andy.
I'll be one up on Andy – he doesn't know my limits but I do!
Many questions running through my head!
The sun was hot and my eyes burned from the glare. I moved,
different angles, and Andy did about 4 sketches. He mentioned
several facial structures compliments and enjoys looking for the
American Indian (Blackfoot) in me. Soon he came in and we
both sat on chairs near the window just a foot apart facing each
other. Now I know how he did Helga's work. The sun is very
crucial to his work. He tried to relax me by saying, "I'm just an
old man, don't pay any attention to me." Somehow, with his blue
eyes, wavy hair and tan it was hard to believe! I think it would
be easier to face a young doctor! Sensing my embarrassment, he
said, "Oh my! Modesty rears its ugly head." With that remark I
felt bolder and more confident because it was true.
Finally he was finished and I got dressed and went to work. I
can't believe I did that!! Even though I bravely told outsiders I
would, if asked to pose nude. Who would turn down an offer
from America's greatest artist? At my age, one thinks of the
immortal aspect and its possibilities.

A week later Helen and George gave Andy a photograph to sign. The pose included Helen's hand on Andy's hand. Andy did so but wiped out part of the original inscription. "We think Betsy might have been hurt or embarrassed in the past and Andy doesn't want to make waves. Who knows? We are still learn-ing!" Helen wrote. Later Helen asked Andy to bring back the photo because she didn't want Andy to hide it from Betsy. Andy objected and said he hung it and likes it.

Andy left his sketchpad in the kitchen and Helen looked at her drawings. She wrote, "The one of me bare-breasted was missing. I didn't recognize myself – maybe because they were sketches."

November 10: We discussed painting me. He marveled at my looks. "You are a beautiful woman. You have a beautiful face. You are vivacious but you are beautiful just like that (looking serious). It will be difficult to do you, to catch that certain glow." Our conversation was intense. The artist was speaking and I knew right then that Andy had great plans for me.

He said our house and us (George and Helen) were his private sanctuary and he didn't want to discuss it with outsiders. Others do not see things as he does and their discussion of his future subjects influences him negatively (Betsy in particular). "I like to let things just happen and if it doesn't turn out it doesn't matter. Others would question, why her? Why that? Why? Why?! Too many questions just lead to more questions." He definitely wants his work and work place private in every way. We will protect him!

He said he wants to do me in a white, flannel nightgown, high neck, maybe buttoned in the back, with maybe a few pleats for shadows in the sunlight. I went upstairs to search for something he thought he had seen on me. He gave me the definite impression that he had been snooping around. I winced at the thought. I brought down several gowns and he said, 'Let's go upstairs – I'll get my sketch pad." He is fascinated with my face and is very expressive. It's strange; I'm flattered but not in the normal way. He offered to pay me for posing and I declined. He said he will do a portrait for me and had other ideas.

Three days later Andy dropped in for a visit and mentioned the Helga and Olsen series sold for $46 million. He said a young man, Peter Marcelle handled the sale. Andy's son Nicky was disappointed that he didn't negotiate the sale. Andy said Nicky was out yachting all summer and didn't do his homework for a transaction.

Andy also told Helen the story of the painting Treading Weeds. Andy said he was recuperating from lung surgery and had his right arm in a sling. He took a walk, looked down and saw these huge feet walking at odd angles (the result of his hip surgery) in the country weeds. "Here I was looking for subjects and there was one literally right at my feet." He marveled at the texture and design of ordinary weeds! With a small fingering motion, he said, some resembled lace. Andy said people miss opportunities right in front of them while looking elsewhere. He amazes himself finding the dynamic beauty of simplistic objects.

During the same visit Andy mentioned some repairs needed to Painter's Folly. "Just have someone do the work," he said. Andy wasn't aware of the couple's financial situation. They were seriously considering re-mortgaging their home to finance the repair work.

> *November 27: Andy told us Betsy cooked Thanksgiving dinner at the schoolhouse. Frolic, Nat and parts of the family were there. Helga is jealous of our photo in Andy's studio and turns it around. Nicky said Andy has a 'new girlfriend,' me. We asked Andy if he would come Xmas for a party and he said yes.*

Helen mailed an invitation to the Wyeths and Andy dropped off Betsy's reply in a sealed envelope. She declined.

> *December 1: Nicely written. We sure are puzzled about their personal life. The true Hollywood scene, we suppose – different lives – different worlds! Do they really get along? Only time will tell.*

As plans were made for the Christmas party, Andy suggested some guests and related a story about Helga. He said two Russians staying with Jamie asked Andy to sign a copy of the book Three Generations. Helga ran outside and snatched the Russians' book saying in German, "No, our book!" Shocked, Andy explained she is Helga and a little eccentric.

About the same time, Joseph Kennedy and his wife visited the Wyeths. They arrived with their two pet falcons.

George penned Betsy a beautiful letter asking her to reconsider attending the party. Helen wondered, "Will she be offended or laugh?" George requested Betsy to "get her ass" to the party. Betsy's secretary was aghast. "Who would write something so daring?" Helen recorded, admiring her husband's creativity. The letter persuaded Betsy to attend the Christmas party.

> *December 10: Since we believed Betsy wasn't going to attend, we dressed a mannequin according to Betsy's style and placed it on*

*a chair at the table. Andy and Betsy arrive! She said she has
brought 'her ass' and is in a merry mood. Andy wore a formal
black and green suit with gold braid from his knighthood in
France to honor Howard Pyle/N. C. Wyeth. Betsy wore a black
dress, black fur hat and silver pod necklace. They gave a bottle
of Dom Perignon '78 vintage. I was truly touched by Andy's
outfit. Jamie wore corduroy pants and navy blazer with three
gold stripes on the bottom of the sleeves and a gold watch in
the lapel of the jacket – very, very military and sophisticated!
A handsome man, warm with a warm smile. We covered a
hanging picture of Andy and us with a drape so not to offend
Betsy. As Betsy passed, Andy remarked, "I really like your
drapes, George!" We all cracked up without Betsy realizing the
joke.
Andy stood and gave a toast and Jamie followed with (another
tribute). Andy remarked to Jamie about the importance of N. C.
Wyeth & Howard Pyle being in this same room and 'now us –
you (my son) and I." Very touching!*

The next day Andy came early to discuss the party with the Sipalas.

*December 11: I wrapped up my vest that was on a mannequin
and added a note: "Dear Betsy: somehow a part of you was
left behind (pardon the pun). Thanks for coming. Much love,
Helen." Andy asked, "Do you really want to do that?" I said,
"No, but I'm going to anyway." I liked the vest. It was unique. I
was hoping she wouldn't be offended. She was impressed by the
vest during the dinner.*
*December 12: Betsy called in early evening and was thrilled with the
vest. She was surprised. She is going to put it together with black
slacks and promised to wear it for me. She said she would like to
meet our children.*

Andy, Nicky and granddaughter Victoria (Nicky's daughter) visited Helen
and George before Christmas and dropped off a Howard Pyle book and a
Christmas wreath as gifts. Helen commented, "I packed up cookies for Victoria.

She is very precocious, very outspoken, mature, affectionate, mannerly and literally came in smiling."

On Christmas Eve, George and Helen dropped off a peach and raspberry trifle at Andy's studio. Betsy was cooking for the family since Phyllis had fallen and injured herself. The Wyeths believed the extra dessert would enhance the family's meal.

CHAPTER TWO
1990

World Premiere

The year 1990 began with an invitation from Andy to attend the world premiere of Treasure Island and a promise to meet the family of Charlton Heston. Heston's son, Fraser, wrote and directed the television version of Robert Louis Stevenson's 1883 novel. In 1911, a Treasure Island book was illustrated by N. C. Wyeth.

January 5, 1990: We are terribly excited and plan new clothes, hair set, car wash. We have no idea what to expect for the evening. Andy said the guest list is growing with lots of notables. Betsy is upset that Heston's wife is coming. She wanted to discuss art with him alone.

January 16: We received our formal invitation. Andy is very excited about the up-coming event. Andy met and immediately liked our son-in-law, Marty Drumheller. They discussed 'old Chadds Ford.' Andy told us about his boxing career. He took a girlfriend and got knocked out right away, never to see the girl again (132-lb weight class). Andy's brother Nat was a good boxer and later took up fencing.

Note: When Nicky and Jamie were small, Andy asked each one what they wanted to be when they grew up. Nicky had his plans and Jamie said he wanted to be a painter "but not like Pop — running through the fields. I want to do something bigger than that." That's when Andy realized Jamie was serious about art.

*Andy said it's a bit scary seeing Jamie's work and knowing Jamie
could surpass him.*

Besides the Treasure Island movie, Andy was involved in another major
artistic project. Andy confided to Helen that a European syndicate was considering donating money to build an addition to the Brandywine River Museum
to house his Helga series. The Japanese might want to make a gift to the United
States, Helen noted. "This was private information."

*January 18: Party night! National History Museum, DE. Saw
    Charlton Heston, his wife, son, Nat Wyeth, Jamie, Phyllis and
    a wide range of Chadds Ford locals along with some du Ponts.
    Good movie! There was applause and a standing ovation. Some
    people gathered around Heston but we stood in the back and
    waited for Andy. He took us up front and introduced us, then
    left hurriedly with Betsy. It made for a short night for us. It took
    us about four days to get over the disappointment of the short
    evening. We expected too much. How silly of us!*

Andy visited several days later to show the Sipalas photographs of *Treasure
Island* that were given to Andy by the Hestons. Andy returned to the widow's
walk to complete the final details of his latest painting, Painter's Folly. Helen
and George hoped to receive a preview of the painting.

*Valentine's Day: Andy dropped off a homemade fudge heart from
    Betsy and a small jar of candy hearts. He left a note saying he
    had a bad leg and had not seen us for a while. Thank goodness,
    a respite! I left him a homemade package of goodies. George and
    I also sent him a Valentine's card. We thought Andy was fading
    us out!*
*March 3: Andy came to visit! A very nice surprise. He wants us to see
    a new painting. A "strange painting," he says.*
*March 4: Andy calls and invites us to the schoolhouse. He greets us
    and rings the school bell. Betsy warmly greets us at the door.
    We drink a mix of champagne and sparkling burgundy. They
    showed us the schoolhouse and old pictures of Painter's Folly.*

> *Betsy suggested taking pictures while we were there. Very nice*
> *of her. Now, the new painting, the "Widow's Walk," is basically*
> *black and white with a sea in the background. He originally*
> *had the Baptist church and the old buttonwood tree in it but*
> *wasn't satisfied and scraped it. He said he had an idea of George*
> *and Helen sailing to Italy. A very large painting and getting*
> *good reviews from Jamie and Nat.*
> *The drink was potent and George and I came home reeling!*
> *What an honor and privilege to be there. We met Jimmy Lynch*
> *(Jamie's childhood friend and an artist) there and the Wyeths*
> *treated us royally.*

Two weeks later, a surprise visit from Andy included a sketching session. Andy said the light was falling perfectly on Helen's face.

> *March 17: My goodness, he does say the most endearing, flirtatious*
> *and bold comments! He truly is enamored with me. He*
> *compliments each part of my face and seems to be moonstruck.*
> *Silly, you say? Believe me! He said Helga and Betsy are aware*
> *that he is attracted to me. I constantly distract him and joke off*
> *his flirting. I wonder if this is part of his subject's familiarity.*
> *I play it straight and laugh a lot. I'm sure he thinks I'm either*
> *naïve or brushing him off. I'm also wondering if he does this*
> *purposely to bring the "glint" in my eyes that he is trying to*
> *capture. Very unusual. For example, he says, "I was attracted to*
> *you from the moment I first saw you. I think of you all the time*
> *and it makes my hand shake even now as I think of you. I wish*
> *I had met you many years earlier – I would be dangerous." On*
> *and on! Andy chats quite freely while working on me. He says he*
> *wants my painting for himself to enjoy.*

Andy dropped in for several visits during the next few weeks without painting. Author Richard Meryman was visiting. Meryman, the son of a painter, worked for Life magazine and authored a book on Andy.

> *March 30: Andy and I go to the 3rd floor where the light is best.*

*Andy does a frontal and side profile. Today Andy shared his
deepest sentiments – revealing beautiful secrets. One of which
was he wanted us to join the Charles Heston dinner but Betsy
objected, stating her friends weren't coming. He says he wants to
give me a painting and another for George and I. I wonder???!!
He promises so much! He dreads Maine and would prefer to
stay here in our company but realizes a family obligation. He is
serious and sad. He hates Maine!*

Andy completed a sketch of Helen. The drawing depicted Helen's neck with a slight twist. Andy was excited about the angle, Helen reported. Later, Andy confided to George that capturing Helen was difficult. If she relaxes too much, she is too stern looking, Andy said. George shared the comment and Helen realized she must cautiously pose in the future.

*April 4: Rain. Andy brings articles about Frolic at Big Bend. We go
to the 3rd floor and Andy describes an outfit he bought for Betsy
for Easter. It would look great on me for the effect he wants in
the painting. He is looking for a high collar and dark color. He
toys with the idea of giving it to me or getting me one like it.
It has a military look with brass buttons. He is also fascinated
with my hands and mentioned several times painting them.*

*April 7: Andy stops in for coffee. He is working at the Craig farm
and obviously feels like he is neglecting us. He is covered with
paint and stays just a short time. Andy reappears with a paint
box in hand to paint me. Our first experience with watercolors.
He works feverishly, slopping water and paint everywhere. The
nice, carefully executed drawing is splashed, dripped, whipped
and rinsed unbelievably so! He pours leftover unwanted water
directly on the hardwood floor. He licks the brushes, leaving
paint on his nose and face. He hastily wipes the painting
with towels and leans the painting on the floor while pouring
water over it to wash off excess colors. His paint supply seems
limited – tubes are spent and he squeezes for the last drops of
desired color. My, is he messy! He wipes brushes on his clothes.
His paint box is slopped alternately with water and paint.*

The paper curls in every direction from all the water wiping.
Strong colors such as dark blue, deep orange, lots of black and
deep yellow are washed into spots, drips and smears. I think,
is this how the master really operates; will this eventually turn
into a masterpiece?? The pencil drawing that he sketched and
erased so diligently, so passionately is quickly disappearing
and a different image appears. Amazing! I feel almost hurt
or offended by his seemingly careless approach to the sketch. I
have put on a bright, white Victorian style blouse with pleats
and ruffles at his suggestion. He is excited and passionate in his
work, complimenting each angle that he sees and is doing at
that precise moment. I can tell where he is by his comments. He
mentions several times that this is only a sketch. But what next?

Helen and George entertained Jane and Forrest Gregory with Andy. The Gregorys lived in Chadds Ford for years. Andy was interested in stories about Painter's Folly and Howard Pyle. Andy encouraged Jane to write a book on her research of the subject.

April 7: He dresses oddly. Pants are about 1 ½" too short (George
thinks 3" and laughs.) He wears a turtleneck, jacket and
trousers in shades of brown, keeping all three of the jacket's
buttons buttoned the complete visit. He looks so strapped! His
chest bone protrudes, he has no behind, spindly legs, big feet,
but an unbelievably handsome tanned face with drooping deep
blue eyes. His gait is both pathetic and comical due to his hip
replacement.

During Easter, Andy, Betsy, Helen and George exchanged food and prank gifts. Helen came down with a cold but Andy insisted on continuing the portrait painting sessions.

April 17: He seems to enjoy talking while painting and encourages me
to do so. I'm not comfortable doing this as I'm afraid of ruining
his concentration. We enjoy learning about each other. He is
fascinated with a black sweater with a high neck for this pose.

*April 20: Andy is finishing up with a pencil sketch. He told me that
Fred Reiter approached Betsy regarding Andy doing nudes at the
Sipalas. We were disgusted and outraged!*

*April 21: Rainy Saturday. He has almost completed this portrait.
It's looking better. He thinks he might have me looking too old.
George and I don't really see a good likeness but maybe it's too
soon. He will try to get Betsy to invite us to Maine but it must
be done "subtlety." He does not want to leave us. Exciting! He is
wheezing in the chest and his nose runs almost continually due
to allergies. I wipe his nose as he paints to prevent dripping on
the painting. We both laugh and he is appreciative.*

*April 23: Came to paint alone. Leaves all of his work on the bed and
floor. Took painting of me home with him. Probably will never
see it again?! Left portfolio here with sketches of Jimmy Lynch,
the Craig farm…It's nice to know he is happy here.*

Andy decided to surprise Betsy by learning how to ride Jimmy Lynch's
motorcycle. When Andy rode off to see Betsy, he was dressed in a black outfit.
George informed Andy he wanted photographs of Betsy's reaction!

*April 24: He just feels like talking a lot and seems so sad about
having to go to Maine. He said the #1 big mistake in his life was
not marrying someone local since he loves the area. He is so fond
of George. Marvels at how fine we both are.*

*April 30: Andy called me at work. When I asked who was calling he
said, "The Shadow." I left work immediately. He said he had the
painting basically finished but needed to look at me again. He
wants to paint my hands and is considering doing a "full body."
Just loves the white blouse with all the lace. It was a good day!*

Andy mastered the motorcycle and drove it to Painter's Folly. He drove
around the driveway twice and tooted but was afraid to stop in case he couldn't
get the vehicle started again.

The next day Helen and Andy discussed George's retirement and the need
of repairs at Painter's Folly and the cost.

May 2: Andy offered to let me work for him selling paintings. He also
offered to help us financially but I politely refused. He asked if
$10,000 would be enough. Can you feature that!! I purposely
changed the subject in rejection.

May 3: Andy brought "White Wash" for us to see, a painting of the
Craig farm. Ha! They didn't get a preview like us!
He paints on a larger piece of paper and erases a lot and has
difficulty getting the feeling on paper. He said it took 3 years to
do Helga. A lot of Helga's work was sketches that were not good
and burned. George hangs a plastic blown-up lady in front of
the 3rd floor window in front of Andy and me. Andy gets a big
kick out of it. We all laugh. George leaves a fake dog mess on the
kitchen floor for Andy. Andy is almost fooled. He had seen one
like it owned by Jamie. Painting session was good.

One of the famous guests of the Wyeth family never made it to Painter's
Folly. Jamie hosted U. S. Senator Ted Kennedy. Andy promised to try to bring
Kennedy for a visit before they went to a point-to-point horse race at Winterthur
Museum, Garden and Library in Delaware. The Sipalas prepared Painter's Folly
but the Senator Kennedy visit never materialized.

May 10: Paint session. Wonderful day. Poured rain and Andy
and I spent a lot of the time in the kitchen over tea revealing
relationship with Betsy. She is good for him but handles the
painting situation like a manager. We mention having his
family over for a birthday dinner. He is frightened and spends
a good portion of the visit telling us why he wants this place
private! They will ruin it for me- He especially feels strongly
about Betsy. She is too "analytical," where as he paints for the
sheer pleasure. He feels the money might have changed her, along
with the Helga episode. His mind wonders and he speaks from
the soul. So personal and touching. In regards to money, he says
he made his money from the "earth beneath my feet." He relates
passionately to items he paints, even touching the very trees,
flowers, etc., as he paints. He resents the approach Betsy takes to
all this: so "calculating and analytical." Her business approach

can sadden and/or impede him.

Andy told Helen he kept her painting in a vault. He wanted additional works of Helen and mentioned taking her to Maine so he could create a nude painting of her in a boat. "Is this just a tease or a test?" Helen wondered.

Another shock for the art world was swirling in Andy's mind. He indicated the surprise might not be unveiled until after his death. Andy didn't disclose to Helen the nature of the shocking collection.

Their conversations included lessons Andy learned during his years as an artist. A major lesson, he related, was not showing a painting until the creation was completed.

> *May 10: Allen Kerstain saw a painting Andy was working on and*
> *mentioned that John Rockefeller would just love it, sight unseen.*
> *Andy finished it and let Allen send it to Rockefeller only to*
> *have him exclaim, "It's not what I expected or had in mind."*
> *Allen then shipped it to Walter Annenberg, who showed some*
> *interest. Upon arrival, Walter saw Rockefeller's name on the old*
> *wrapping and refused to even look at it! End of sale!*
> *Another lesson. When (a man's) wife saw her husband's partially*
> *painted portrait, she thought it horrible. When finished and*
> *husband died, she cherished it and hangs it above her fireplace.*
> *She apologized many times for such negative comments.*

During the month of May, Andy brought good news to the Sipalas. White Wash was sold and Widow's Walk was part of a new show at the Brandywine River Museum.

> *May 18: George and I dress and go to the museum to see "Widow's*
> *Walk." Our guide says the painting was done in Maine. The*
> *guide didn't know us. Andy arrives. He puts on a seaman's coat*
> *that Charlton Heston wore in Treasure Island. I try on the coat*
> *and we laugh about its history. He takes the coat and drives off*
> *and doesn't wave. He has plans but, as usual, is very secretive. I*
> *feel like he has left me in the lurch. I thought he was just putting*
> *the coat in the car. Sometimes I feel his age takes over in some*

strange actions. Terribly independent!

May 19: Andy brings the coat for George to see. A lively visit – maybe to make up for the hasty departure yesterday. Note: At some point he started waving as he drives away. We always stood by the door until he was out of sight. He also has a heavy foot in pulling out, sometimes skidding on the lawn. I do believe he sincerely loves us and the precious visits. Such a break for him. Such joy and thrills for us!

Andy arrived at Painter's Folly and was excited about a luncheon invitation to the Russian Embassy. He wanted Helen to join him if Jamie wasn't available to do so. Jamie did attend. "Truly, Andy was handsome this day and we took pictures," Helen wrote. "I wish I were going with him."

Helen and George did receive invitations to another social event. They were excited about being asked to attend a gathering at Frolic Weymouth's home. Helen recorded, "We are in ecstasy! A dinner party at Frolic's at 7 p.m."

June 8: Andy called to see if I got my hair cut. He remembered my hair appointment. Can you imagine? What did he have in mind? He said he would be right over and I put on a wig and played a joke on him. He said it was "cute." Then I pulled off the wig. Lots of laughs! He wants to paint me in the widow's walk in the moonlight. He said he would be back that night if it was a clear night. It was raining. We went to bed. He drives up and bounds in with a bottle of wine like it's party time! He goes upstairs, wakes George and the three of us check out the widow's walk. We sit there waiting for the moon to rise above the trees. He is ecstatic with the painting possibilities and chastises us for not using the room for observing the moon from such a vantage point. "It takes Andy Wyeth to teach you such things," he said. He is dreaming of winter painting with a heater. Our future looks secure.

While waiting for the moon in the widow's walk, Andy told a story of a man stopping at his house while looking for gas. Andy took the man to a gas station and drove him back to the man's stranded Cadillac. Andy didn't introduce himself but the man said, "Thanks, Mr. Wyeth." The next day Andy received a note stating the man had planned to rob him but he liked Andy and couldn't commit the crime. He warned Andy never to make himself vulnerable again. Helen wrote, "A chilling story!"

Andy returned the next night and painted until 2 a.m. He was to be a dinner guest at the Sipalas' home the next night but left a message that he had a fever from sitting in the late night air painting and couldn't attend. He also asked for a thermometer.

> *June 11: I went down alone. He was burning up (102 degrees). I put cold wash clothes on his head, took chicken soup and stayed awhile. He didn't want Betsy or anyone else to know. She might come home from Maine. He was entertaining the idea of sleeping at our house to keep the secret.*
> *June 12: I called Andy and he is a little better. He invites George and I down. He is in bed (temp. 101). We take him Tasty Freez ice cream. We sit in his bedroom and chat.*

After Andy recovered from his cold, Helen and George hosted a dinner party for some of the Wyeth family.

> *June 17: Funny stories were told. Andy crawled under the table and Jamie gave a surprise. Burgundy champagne flowed freely. Strangely, we all ate lightly. Andy, Jamie and I toured the yard and they saw the mermaids. I had difficulty getting them in the house to eat. A great night for us all!*
> *June 20: I called Andy to invite him for fish dinner; joked with him about beets only to discover I was talking to Richard Meryman from the "Post" magazine. George and I both guessed they would show up within an hour and they did. Surprise! They brought a plate of cooked beets. Meryman was an interesting man. I took his phone # before he left. Will the surprises never end?? Such contacts! Andy is so excited and proud of us. Thrilling!*

Helen and George spent a weekend in South Carolina with Andy caring for their dog, Gilda.

Andy was vague about his own annual travel to Maine. Andy planned to stay in Pennsylvania until after the 4th of July but departed early for Maine when Betsy suffered a cut to her leg. Helen wrote, "Everything is up in the air! He is so secretive. And not everything he says is straightforward. He doesn't always tell you the whole story. Is he used to hiding and fooling people?"

Andy returned to Pennsylvania for his brother Nat's funeral on July 9. Andy rented a plane to fly relatives from Maine for the services. Nat died on July 4 at age 78. The service was held at a crowded Church of the Advent on a hot day. Helen and George attended. Andy then invited Helen and George to a dinner that evening at the Dilworthtown Inn with Wyeth family and friends. "Pleasant surprise!" The dinner included Jean Wyeth, Ann McCoy, McCoy's daughter Anna B. McCoy who had married Frolic Weymouth, Meryman and Pam, a model.

> *July 9: I gave a toast to Nat and then we all sang Happy Birthday to Andy. George dressed up as a woman to surprise Andy. I had music on a tape. Skit didn't go real well at the table.*
>
> *July 18: Andy called. Andy mentions that the skit didn't go well with his nieces and Pam. 'Poor taste and bad timing' was the feedback. No wonder they were so somber. Andy is so frank with me that it is shocking. He defends George. Even though I tell him I'm not telling George, I called George immediately after hanging up. This is serious stuff! He is also stressed that Ann left early, indicating the skit was the reason. Bad timing for a birthday surprise.*
> *George and I review an apology letter that George wrote. A good letter.*
>
> *July 20: Andy calls again. I mention the letter and he wants to hear it. He is impressed and congratulates George on such a beautiful thought and letter.*

The July 9 dinner also included intrigue between Pam and Helen. During the dinner, Pam made a play for Andy and told Helen that she will "fight for him." Helen told Pam that she could have him. Other Wyeth family undercurrents took place at the dinner.

> *July 20: Andy called because he is "lonely" but is it really to discuss*
> *the skit feedback? I feel so terrible that this all happened. Thank*
> *God that George and I can stick it out together and feel secure*
> *that Andy will remain loyal. Andy, George and I all wait for*
> *the apology feedback. P. S. Andy and I spend some time on the*
> *phone arguing and bantering, he loves to fight with me because*
> *I'm absolutely frank and down to earth with him. We both howl*
> *with laughter. He confirms the pleasure he receives.*

After returning to Maine, Andy called Helen and George about once a week.

> *August 15: Andy called and said it was rough being up there. He*
> *is looking for an excuse to come back soon. Betsy's leg still has*
> *not healed. He is happy to hear my voice and laughter, a sign*
> *of homesickness. I could tell he is lonely for his unfinished*
> *paintings and happy surroundings.*

Andy returned in late August. In October Helen and George joined him for dinner at the Dilworthtown Inn. "Great time," Helen wrote. "Andy and I have a few minutes of serious talk. I'm sitting on his right again. He 'loves my innocence,' so he says."

On October 24, Andy was awarded the Congressional Gold Medal by President George H. W. Bush during a ceremony at the White House. President Bush said Andy's paintings "caught the heart of America." The gleaming medal, made of nearly pure gold by the U.S. Mint, featured a picture of Andy that was created by Jamie. The next day Andy brought the medal to show George and Helen.

> *October 25: Andy & Nicky came to show the Washington medal. We*
> *wore white gloves to handle. Andy says he is ordering a similar*
> *one. A short visit.*
> *October 27: Andy stopped in and left a witch sketch. He also left*
> *a pumpkin on the kitchen table. We missed him. I sprinkled*
> *powder on the 3rd floor stairs and we could see his footprints. He*
> *had been sketching.*

October 28: Enjoyable morning. Andy said he would pay for our tickets to the New York show. (Peter Marcelle, a New York gallery owner who championed Andy's works, hosted the one-person show). Tickets are $125 each. What a predicament! We don't have the money to go but can't accept his. He wants us to go. How will we handle this?? He had an invitation sent to us. Oh! My!

October 31: Halloween. Andy came dressed as a witch with black cape, hat and wig. He invited us to George Hebner's house for a bonfire party. George drove his jeep. Andy came in the house afterwards and went to the widow's walk. Fun evening!

George and Helen did receive an invitation to Andy's New York show and they attended.

November 15: Saw Frolic who introduced us to Mrs. Rockefeller. We took the train and walked part way to the gallery. A beautiful trip and night. So exciting! Marcelle said Andy called regarding the turnout and Marcelle stated that the Rockefellers were there but Andy was more interested in the Sipalas being there. Marcelle was aghast and we were totally flattered! We also saw Eric (Standard) who posed nude for Andy ("The Clearing").

November 16: Andy came with a National Geographic photographer in our absence. George and I had placed a dummy on the kitchen floor; a chair turned over and dressed in George's clothes. We planned this for several days but wanted to be there to witness it. String attached to the arm would have given the dummy some movement. Andy jumped 2 feet and the photographer was scared enough to suggest calling the police. A very good joke! Andy said to his guest, "You have to know these people."

During November Andy painted Helen and dropped in for numerous chats and tea. While painting and chatting with Helen, George took the opportunity to put a "Just Married" sign on Andy's car. He drove off without seeing it. Andy received a number of comments about George's handiwork.

Helen spent time planning a Christmas party for Andy, her second one.

Betsy indicated she would attend the dinner party.

> *December 8: I was frantic preparing dinner for the Sunday*
> *Christmas party and was mortified to see Andy. Wasn't a good*
> *day for posing but the master calls and you go with the mood.*
> *Does he realize the work involved with entertaining?*
> *December 9: Big day! Xmas party. 7 p.m. Guests: Betsy, Andy,*
> *Mimi and Harry Haskell, Bill and Tish Hewitt, Nejma and*
> *Peter Beard (famed writer, photographer and artist), Kathy*
> *and Frolic Weymouth, Jamie and George Bronfman's wife.*
> *Bronfman is Seagram's 7 heir and a large stockholder of*
> *DuPont. Jamie called one hour before dinner to ask permission*
> *to bring her. Table was set for Nicky who didn't come. Easy*
> *transfer. I read a quote from the Pitz book of Howard Pyle: 'a*
> *unique moment' instead of a prayer. Richard DiBlazio played*
> *the accordion for one hour during dessert. All applauded.*
> *George dressed in a "Wobbie" Halloween outfit. Peter Beard*
> *took pictures during dinner. I gave a box of homemade truffles*
> *to each guest. Betsy and Andy gave us a copy of N. C. Wyeth's*
> *letters (book) and signed it for us. The evening was a blast. Andy*
> *said, "A surprise every minute."*
> *December 10: Andy called, "Everyone just loved it, a lovely party!"*

The week before Christmas Helen and George gave Andy a beret like the one George wore. "Andy looked charming in his hat but we don't think he'll continue to wear it. He doesn't usually wear one," Helen wrote. Andy surprised Helen with a miniature Congressional Medal and a black cord in a gray velvet case, just like the one Betsy owns. Helen wrote, "A beautiful surprise! Betsy was not to know, as she was the only other person to have one. George and I were thrilled!"

> *December 27: Andy came in a long black coat and George's Xmas*
> *hat. He retired to the 3rd fl. to paint. We lit a kerosene heater*
> *early to warm up the room. Good conversation and confirmed*
> *friendship. He is so happy to share our home and love."*

CHAPTER THREE
1991

Andy Shares His Soul

Andy celebrated New Year's Day with Helen and George with a bottle of wine but he didn't stay too long as his foot was hurting him. Snow blanketed Chadds Ford early in January but the weather didn't keep Andy from Painter's Folly, the Sipalas and his painting.

January 16: Andy painted me using water colors. He wanted all my makeup off, realizing this was a hindrance in his initial painting of me. A fruitful session. I wore my usual white Victorian blouse. He loves me in white. His dream is to take me to a Washington formal, buying a white gown in West Chester. I don't dream like him and put little faith in it. In my mind it's very remote! Is it a carrot? He fantasizes a lot anyway. He loves to dance and dress up.

Note: I am getting tests for high blood pressure and/or a heart problem. I definitely feel the excitement, anxiety, suspense and joy with his visits. It has been a long (or short?) two years of fun and surprises. Each visit adds a new dimension to our newly found friend and our lives. I feel when it snows that he comes to visit just to get charged for his paintings since he attributes the success of the "Widow's Walk" to us and our home. He is so

*proud of that painting and had an offer of $5,000,000. He has
received new, fresh reviews for the painting.*

Andy's numerous visits to the Sipalas caused some wild speculation among Helen's "nosey neighbors!" During one visit, Andy showed Helen a letter from a concerned woman. "It mentioned my name and was concerned that Andy was here so often. She had no idea of Andy's studio being here and the amount of painting being done. We all got a laugh out of it," Helen recorded.

*January 31: How long is this going to take before we see a final
product? He moves from one window to the next, from one
sketch to another! Maybe he just enjoys the chats on a rainy day.*
*February 7: He paints but is terribly excited about doing me in the
widow's walk. He wants me in the white blouse against the
stark windows and pure white walls. He realized something
was missing in all my poses and is like a child with a new toy!
He can't wait for a sunny day now. What will I do with sunny
and rainy days off from work! No pay! Oh! My! He is so happy
at this stage.*

Andy's sessions were interrupted as his sister Carolyn suffered a stroke. The painting restarted on Valentine's Day.

*February 15: Not much sun. Painted awhile and then he took me on
a tour of Kuerner's hills. It was a fun day for us both. Jamie fell
off his bike and fractured his left arm. He is in the hospital.*
*February 16: Good painting session in widow's walk. Andy is so very
excited! It's going to be a good painting, just wait and see! An
hour after he left, I went to bed. Aching all over. The posing
position, which was two pillows on a bucket with nothing to
lean on, straight position is making my tailbone sore. Actually
was coming down with a virus and didn't know it.*
*February 17: I'm in bed sick and he goes to widow's walk alone to
work. George and I were both in bed when we heard him come
in. Gads! That was too early! See how excited he is. He sits
on my bed and visits awhile. Funny jokes and laughs! Betsy*

discussed pleasure with my posing. She is enthused also. Andy feels good about it all.

February 18: Andy didn't expect us to be home. He brings a basket of oranges for me. George and I are in bed. I'm still recovering and George has a holiday from work. Our love session is broken by the sound of Andy's voice. George runs down the back stairs and pretends to be up and around. Little does Andy know! Andy sits on my bed and chats awhile. Carolyn might go to a convalescent home. Jamie had a room across the hall from her in the hospital.

Andy honored Helen and George by showing them his latest painting, Home. They were the first persons to see the finished work.

February 22: Widow's walk. Good session. He loves the long black skirt. He brings watercolors and the paintings comes alive. I'm happy with the results. He is excited about the location, light, and shadows: all the things that are particularly "Wyeth!" We stand by the window in the widow's walk and marvel at the view and our home.

February 23: I fixed coffee and got the house warm. He painted and later came down for tea. We put Amaretto in our tea and enjoyed very casual conversation. Andy teased that he feels the liquor in the tea and pretends to stagger out the door. He surprises us by circling the driveway once before leaving, as if in confusion. A great joke! He truly is young at heart. He is on his way to see Carolyn at the hospital. He mentions painting me nude when the weather gets warmer. I hope not as I don't respond.

February 24: Coffee first, as usual, with doughnuts. Andy says Carolyn is very confused at times, thinking she is in Maine. He paints in the widow's walk and after hinting and ultimately asking me, I pose in half nude. A very different, difficult and embarrassing experience. I protest that I don't have Helga's figure and am uncomfortable with the idea. I slip on my robe and slippers, sit on a stool and modestly show an in inch at a time to the waist. Really Embarrassing! He has

*to be disappointed with my figure. I give him credit for his
consideration for my modesty. He told me to just remember that
he is only an old man and an artist. He keeps sketching and
closes his eyes when I ease down the robe. We both laugh and
ease into the situation. It is tolerably warm and both heaters
are on. We have a nice talk about the arts, personal secrets and
our2-year friendship. He loves it here and feels so comfortable
and at home. He says he will pay me for posing after the
painting is finished. Who knows! He has no idea of my aching
back many times, lost wages, excuses at work and days of not
feeling too good. Such a loss of privacy and morning freedom.*

A news article riled Andy. He commented he dreamt of bowing out of
the art scene so Jamie could be independent. The article compared Jamie with
Andy. Betsy believed the article was positive but Andy sided with Jamie and
feared for Jamie's emotional state. Andy's dreams took him to Europe or on a
ship or any place to just disappear. He felt he was a hindrance to Jamie. "Andy
reveals his most deep and treasured secrets and I feel he is sharing a part of his
soul with me. A very emotional and serious side of Andy. I feel sad with and for
him. I don't sleep well after the visit," Helen wrote.

*February 28: Andy comes with pockets full of money. He sold a
painting and still is carrying the cash. What a wad! George and
I are hopeful when he says he has come to pay his model. He
is in high spirits. The excitement is at a fever pitch. He comes
almost every day and I get nervous. (Helen has to make excuses
at work for being late.)*
*March 2: I can't believe it, here he is again! He has too much pink on
my face in the painting (I forgot to take off my makeup) and it
bothered him last night. He wanted to see me natural, I suppose.
Frolic is in the hospital for a heart by-pass and Andy, George
and I send him a joke wrapped in a box.*
*March 3: Frolic called from the hospital to say he would be here on
March 28th for dinner. He's getting a balloon heart operation.*
*March 6: He has great plans for a series of me and is thinking of a
moonlit pose in the widow's walk. He is very excited and full of
plans.*

March 9: A very long session and my shoulder blades hurt!

On the second Sunday in March, Andy arrived early and hustled Helen into the widow's walk to catch the sunrays. The session was a long one but Andy was able to inspire his model. Helen wrote, "He gets me all fired up with a silly sexual accusation, my eyes are flashing in defense and he is overjoyed; he has the look in my eyes necessary for the final touches in the painting. We sit on the floor about two feet apart and I realize how he does the fine exact detail close up. The master is truly at work!"

March 11: Note: Our morning visits (George, Andy and me) over coffee are always full of naughty jokes, the latest gossip, news (national and local) and, as usual, very personal news of his family. Andy is so free with his personal news and confides in us completely.

March 17: A beautiful day. Time was spent sitting on the floor getting a close-up for face detail. We went outside on the front porch to sit in the sun. Took pictures and Andy was relaxed and jovial. Fun!

March 19: I passed by my house on the way to Kennett Square. I surprised Andy and he immediately wanted me to pose for a while. The time was perfect for him and he appreciated it.

March 20: I think Andy is a dreamer and a fantasizer. He thrives on Camelot stories, folklore, ancient quotes, Robin Hood, etc. I confront him as a dreamer and he says his dreams come true. It's a serious conversation and I am left disillusioned as to the serious side of him. I believe he fibs at will and the truth is hard to pinpoint, even when he pleads serious and wants to be convincing. I think much of his excitement, promises and dreams are done for the benefit of a good painting. He has to be on a "high" to be productive. Am I wrong?

March 24: Andy was here when we returned from church. He erases my face in the painting! He wasn't happy with it. Just as well as we weren't that thrilled either, little did he know. He told me to go buy a stunning dress and he would pay for it. "Knock them dead." I started shopping like crazy! Never looked at price tags.

He is anxious to show us off. It was supposed to be our secret regarding the dress.

The dinner party took place March 28. Helen's decorations included live caged parakeets on the dining room table with fresh pansies and flowers down the center of the table. Those attending included Andy, Betsy, Frolic and five other people. Helen wore a plain black dress that the Wyeths told her was "STUNNING!"

April 7: The painting is coming along nicely and Andy and I are pleased. We discuss it from a distance. He invites honesty. I tell him what I feel which I know happens to be what he wants to hear. I feel comfortable in expressing my views, which are all complimentary. Sincerely so. I do love the painting. It's going to be a hit! We discuss the du Pont families, his models, Helga at length, the trips to Maine, Carolyn Wyeth and her bad luck as a teenager and their closeness as brother and sister. I reinforce my feelings about the "man" and the Wyeth painter. I want him to know that I love him as a friend but not to the point of adulation. I don't want him to think he's a god. How do I write this correctly? I also want him to know our friendship is sincere and not devious. We sit awhile without painting and chat about serious and funny family situations. He feels resentful about Betsy using him as a vessel or commodity, re: the paintings. He wants to work freely and feels that the Helga period was a result of some frustrations. He wants me to have my painting if anything happens to him. I voice some skepticism and claim that his family will take everything. He says he will put it in writing. Who knows!??

April 8: I stay only a few minutes. I say I will blow my horn when leaving. As I do, I see him on the roof, shirt off (he almost looks naked) waving … the funniest sight ever!

April 10: He says he only comes to finish some cloud detail. When we come home Andy has left a note "a surprise is on the 2nd floor." He wanted George to be the 1st to see it, an honor! It is all temporarily matted and framed. We are so pleased.

> *April 11: He spends the morning finishing. He speaks to its
> "freshness" and the fact that the setting is unique. I say I
> look younger in it and he says I really look that way to him.
> "Regal" is a much-used word with him and he has always been
> impressed with my posture. He reframes the painting. He truly
> is thrilled with the results. After much celebration we go down
> and have tea, bringing the painting with us.*
>
> *April 12: Betsy Wyeth called to marvel about the painting. She loves
> the water in the background. What water? The title is "The
> Glass House." She'll have us down to see it when it is finally
> framed. Jamie loves it. Betsy thinks it looks like her mother, tall
> and regal. A pleasant call. Why shouldn't they be pleased, it's
> probably worth a million!*

On April 12, Helen and George rode in an elegant carriage with Frolic
Weymouth. George took photographs to record the event. Helen's description
included the fact "three or four dogs led the way through fields of bluebells and
yellow wildflowers." She recorded the weather as a cool 65 degrees necessitating
the occupants to wear wool dress, jackets, hats and gloves. "We all look dapper!"
Helen commented. Midway through the ride, they stop and all had a drink.
After the ride, Frolic showed a video of his 1985 Buckingham Palace coach ride.
"What a delightful evening," according to Helen.

> *April 12: George and I go shopping and I experience the most
> unusual sadness overwhelming me. I felt like I had been
> pregnant, gave birth and gave the baby up for adoption –
> postpartum. Andy and I worked on the "Glass House" painting
> for a year. Sure, he had other work at the same time and there
> were periods of slow down and summers in Maine but sketching
> always continued. Now the painting is lost to the world, matted
> and sealed permanently. "Glass House" is gone and a lot of me
> with it!*
>
> *Another feeling: I always separated Andy from his art world mentally
> and verbally. To us he was just a wonderful friend. I couldn't
> stand being reminded of his worldly status and the importance
> of his work…It took away from a meaningful relationship in*

the more natural way. But now, suddenly, I realize the reality of
it all. The most famous American artist just painted me! Wow!
Very sobering.

Andy visited Helen the next day, surprising his model. Helen told Andy of her sad feelings about the completion of the painting. When Andy revealed his sketch pad and pencils, Helen was cheered and thought, "Here we go again!"

April 13: He wants to be sure he has my nose right. We discuss the
painting, people's reactions, future work and our friendship. He
mentions that Helga carries a manuscript with her recounting
his statements and feelings about his paintings. He said he
peeked while she left the studio. Evidently, she is writing a book
regarding him. I say nothing of my own diary as he might be
trying to test me.
Note: There is so much more I could record but when he leaves and I
race to work and record maybe a week or two later, I forget so
much of the intimate talks. I'm not doing a good job recording.

During the next sketching session, Helen wore a red jacket and black skirt she purchased in Spain. She posed in front of different windows at Painter's Folly and Andy sketched a little. They spent a good deal of the time talking about dreams.

April 16: I show him a poem, "A Dreamer." I read it to him but
I have to emphasize that I approve of it or he gets defensive.
Betsy often criticizes this aspect of him. Good paintings are
his dreams and also the result of them. I repeat that I always
separate him from his paintings because that's a side of Andy
I'm not familiar with. He corrects me by adding "a side you're
afraid of." I say, "Yes, thank you." I really don't enjoy opening
myself up to a famous person. How would they know how I live,
my joys or heartaches, my social life, my family, how can they
relate? How sincere could this relationship be? Only time will
tell what we mean to him or his friends and family. He says he
has been writing a diary all his life and the entries are coded in

> *hieroglyphics and hidden away. Is this part of his "dreams" or*
> *is he trying to find out if I'm writing also? I'm not going to be*
> *caught in his play. If he finds out, he might be more cautious*
> *in his openness. Andy has a unique ability to express himself.*
> *He has a great memory and is so sensitive and so passionate*
> *in his zest for life. I feel this is connected to his artistic and*
> *dramatic talents, especially for someone with limited formal*
> *education. How many times has he been this open with anyone?*
> *I'm cautious and he has always sensed this about me. It's so*
> *hard to distinguish between fact and fiction with him and I'm*
> *constantly on guard.*

Andy concluded the session by discussing Betsy's health and her evening cocktails. Andy departed in Carolyn's car as Helga was using his car to take Carolyn to the hospital.

> *April 27: A real surprise! I didn't expect him. I felt he just wasn't into*
> *the sketching yet. He had been to Granogue (du Ponts) and was*
> *all revved up to start painting again. He asked me to be patient*
> *and bear with him. He wants to do several paintings of me*
> *until the world "knows my soul." He is interested in a close up*
> *portrait, something like Helga, I suppose. He mentions again*
> *that I have been good to him. I know that he would love to see*
> *me enjoy some of the fame and glory associated with his models.*
> *He says he dreams, thinks and plans constantly of positions,*
> *lighting and background.*
> *I tell him my episode with the garage door falling and my nerves*
> *falling to pieces with George's anger. Lots of tears yesterday. He*
> *listens sympathetically and reassures me. I think he finds it hard*
> *to understand the real impact of George's anger on me, the past*
> *damage and anguish! We talk at great length. He is comforting.*

Andy and Helen and George exchanged May baskets, given in secret. Andy's basket had a note from "Robin Hood." Helen and George dropped off their reciprocal basket, which included flowers and some tadpoles with a note reading, "spring brings new life. May Day is for sharing."

May 4: He feels I'm an elusive person and I retort with his being an elusive butterfly … always flitting around. He disagrees with me. I picture him as a butterfly with black wing tips, shades of brown turning to cream, yellow and maybe a speck of red. He sees me as a brilliant red one. Such silly banter! We talked of nature, flowers, the earth and what we have in common. We both feel good after such a talk.

May 7: We discuss various topics. Little does he know that I find it difficult to believe so much of what he says. Why does he do that? (Lie, fabricate, fluff, etc.) Is it a life-long habit connected to clandestine living? Does he do this to reach the psyche of his models? Many things leave me uneasy and I will question him the next time. He says he is completely open with me but I find him evasive and contradictory and it all makes me cautious with my output of information. When I sense he's not honest I feel like he's treating me like a child, due to our age differences and maybe he sees me as gullible. I must be careful not to express my disbelief as often as I feel it. But then I look gullible. What a crazy friend! He and Betsy both see me as the strength in the household. Now that's a real twist!! She thinks George is such a sweet person.

As Andy prepared for a new show at the Brandywine River Museum and the introduction of Helen's painting, he mused over the next painting of Helen.

May 14: He has been dreaming of new poses. I try on a black skirt, white blouse, black stockings and then remove each one until I am nearly naked. Maybe it was planned but I hardly think so. He is not pleased with the nearly naked pose saying I am a regal lady and wants me to stay that way. He doesn't want to repeat the Helga bit! He wants one door fixed in the Painter's Folly because it won't close and he doesn't want Helga barging in, which is very much like her.

May 16: Andy has some big stories. He said he gave Betsy a painting for their anniversary that had been hanging in his studio. Helga asked where it was and after he told Helga, Helga flew out of the

house and left in her car. Sensing something, Andy followed her.
Helga went to the school house and demanded the painting from
Betsy, saying Andy gave it to her. Andy pulled up and told Helga
to "get the hell off the porch and leave." Andy was proud of his
own reaction and feels it helped Betsy understand the Helga
situation. We discuss his relationship with Seri and Helga.
Interesting! Also models Pam and Dee. He has strong convictions
about his models.

When the Glass House was hung at the Brandywine River Museum, Helen and George had a special escort, Andy.

May 18: I felt like I was going to be operated on as we rode the
elevator. As we started down the hall I felt like I was going to
a viewing! Eerie! A very strange feeling for me, indeed. Andy
discussed several of his paintings and a few people started to
notice him.
An elderly couple stopped him. The gentleman said he thought
Karl Kuerner (a former World War I soldier who modeled for
Andy) killed his father in the war. A very unusual conversation.
Andy slipped away gently with directness, never looking back. It
was such an honor to be with him. Absolutely awesome! To think
we know him like we do!

The trio went back to Painter's Folly to discuss the painting. Andy did another sketching session with Helen. Helen believed the adjustments to her face made her jaw more slender. Helen gently told Andy of the comments by her children and he agrees with them. The children thought the look on Helen's face is too stern and she is prettier than depicted. Friends said they were disappointed with the painting. One stated, "He isn't your friend. He doesn't love you for the way he painted you." Other comments included that Helen looked stern, grouchy, old and ugly. "We are all getting a little gun shy because he is so far off in capturing the face. I try to be gentle with him," Helen wrote.

May 24: Andy said, "You have no idea what I'm going to do for you.
I will make you so famous the whole world will know you." He

doesn't want to do me nude but elegantly sensual – a different approach from the "regal" position. He has a high respect for me and is honored to be here. He wants the leotards without underpants as he doesn't want the lines to interrupt the free flowing legs. He's right.

May 25: He said he has three legitimate buyers for "Glass House" and expresses a bit of defiance, like it's still a good painting and very saleable, regardless of what people say.

May 26: We went to church. When I returned I went upstairs and Andy was lying on my posing bed with my leotards on, stretching out in my posing position to the "T!" The funniest thing you could see. Quite a joke! He has serious chats about his dreams, artwork, commitments and the present painting. I tell him the children think I have aged a lot in the last five years. He is disgusted and says none of my daughters look as good as me. "Wait until they see this painting," he retorts. I assure him it's ok and just a family custom to criticize. He invites us to the schoolhouse for the stop-in we requested to present his early birthday gift. We gave Betsy and Andy handmade cloth dolls with their faces from photographs. They loved them. We didn't stay. I am not too comfortable around Betsy since we have so much information not to be shared with her. They have a funny relationship.

May 27: Andy is still bothered that my kids said I'm looking older. He says this next painting will be "ageless!" He loves it up in the room and takes his shoes and shirt off while painting.

May 29: Andy here alone. Got a lot done on the minor sketches. He locks the door downstairs and up in the room to keep Helga and others out while painting. She definitely has an alarming hold on him, but he is embarrassed to admit her strength and his weakness.

May 30: He looks handsome in his blue dress shirt, green dress slacks and his nice boat shoes. I pose briefly semi-nude without the leotards so he can get a better idea of flesh.

Andy's conversation subject turned to the future. He was adamant Helen was to keep his works in Painter's Folly if he dies. He was especially concerned about his death when he was flying. Andy said he was "just a spirit" and wanted to leave this world that way. He would like to be thrown overboard from a ship, not placed in the ground and not have a funeral service. Betsy will be buried in Maine with her parents, Andy said, and he doesn't want to be in the Birmingham cemetery with Nat. It's in his will, so he told Helen. He wasn't sure if Betsy would carry out his wishes.

He was scheduled to go to Maine with Betsy on June 1 for a week. Andy planned, Helen wrote, to return "for me, Frolic, Carolyn, his ear problems and a month of marathon carousing."

One disclosure by Andy stunned Helen. Andy confided that Betsy thought a lot of Helen and believed Helen to be "very natural and attractive."

> *May 30: I am shocked, as Betsy lives in another world as far as I am concerned. I can't fathom her having an opinion one way or another. Betsy said I am a beautiful woman and Andy answered, "Yes, but in an odd way." He can't have her bothered by the whole situation and has to minimize it. He was a bit surprised by her feelings and he felt (Betsy) was giving her stamp of approval.*

Andy returned from Maine on June 7 as scheduled and in his trademark spirited form. Helen found Andy and George sprawled on the kitchen floor with a vodka bottle. "A real prank! "Andy is so good at acting," Helen wrote. "He doesn't move a muscle or go out of position even though laugher has taken over. I am so glad to see him. I jump on top of him on the floor and playfully beat on him. He looks great and loves the attention. His hair is a bit longer on top of his head like I like it. He has such beautiful curly hair and he looks so much older with a crew cut. I just love this man with his laughter, energy and goofiness walking on stilted legs!"

The reunion concluded when Andy departed to spend family time at Jamie's home. He did return to Painter's Folly later in the evening. Nicky's family was visiting and Andy wanted to spend the night with Helen and George.

> *June 7: We laugh ourselves silly at the thought and I fix up the master*

> *BR. Andy climbs into bed with his clothes on. George puts on
> his red-striped nightgown and matching nightcap and I wear
> a nightgown and robe. Who would believe that the three of us
> are in bed together like three kids? We joke and marvel at the
> thought of Chadds Ford gossip. We reminisce about Howard
> Pyle, the history of the house, laugh a lot and finally get sleepy.
> George and I return to our room but sleep very little, as the
> experience was both exhilarating and unbelievable!*
> *June 8: At about 6 am I hear Andy going to the 3rd floor. He peaks
> in our room and I wave him in. He lies on top of the covers,
> George wakes up and we begin more stories and laughter. When
> he gets up I am aware that his eyes are searching for art poses. I
> can see it in his eyes.*

Helen and George attended Frolic's preview party for his art show at the Brandywine River Museum. Andy was there with Helga and Jean Wyeth. The event drew a large crowd and food and drink were abundant.

> *June 8: Helga kisses George and leans over to me but I shake her
> hand. I am awestruck to hear her speak and be so natural. No
> running or hiding this time, a shock to me. I am struck by her
> almost homeliness, her heavy body, the denim jacket and skirt,
> white flat boots, the braided hair on either side of her head and
> pulled to the top of her head. Did Andy make her attractive in
> his paintings? Others crowd in and George and I slip away. He
> tells us to keep the bed warm.*

The preview elicited varied comments on Helen's painting. "It's fabulous! I wish he would paint me," was one of the positive remarks. Other comments were critical. Some patrons thought Andy didn't capture Helen's spirit or vitality and tried to make Helen look like the same age as Andy. Others were more neutral, saying Andy as an artist has the right to paint as he feels and what he sees, not as other people see Helen. When asked about her thoughts, Helen said, "It's not a photograph and maybe not as people see me but Andrew Wyeth painted it and it's hanging in the museum. I'm thrilled!"

Helen admitted feeling shy about the painting. "Is it because it all seems so personal?" Helen and George left the preview party "a little disenchanted."

June 10: He is anxious today and compassionate. He is aware that
we were left out of the after parties while he danced and lived
it up. Betsy, in Maine, is mad at him because he took Helga.
She thought it was planned. She was really upset! He is very
perceptive and senses I am pained by it all. He delicately and
compassionately tries to cover up, apologize and smoothes things
over, saying we are good friends, a good model and he didn't
want to lose me. I try hard not let on but I did feel left out, no
doubt about it. He guesses my thoughts. Amazing!

Three days in a row Andy worked at Painter's Folly. On June 14, Andy stubbed his toe on the end of the bed and fell into his paint box. Helen commented, "What a mess! I refuse to look."

June 15: Andy is pleased with the progress of the painting. The face
seems better and not so stern. He says Helga won't go to dinner
with me. Andy says she thinks I don't like her, that I didn't give
her a kiss at the party and she's jealous.
Note: Betsy asks about me again. He tells her that he shared her
compliments with me and that I was touched.
June 16: He comes full of regret and frightful thoughts of hurting our
feelings. Painting is difficult for him today. He is emotional. He
thinks this house is a "goldmine."

Andy asked to stay overnight at Painter's Folly. Helen wrote, "I realized why he has come to sleep here. He is caught up with the excitement of the house; its history, his mission here, our friendship and future possibilities. He is awed by it all."

June 18: A really good dinner. We listen to classical music and Andy
lies on the couch, eyes closed in enjoyment and plays with my
toes while I sit on one end of the couch. The three of us critique
each composition and enjoy it to the fullest. He leaves satisfied as
a kitten.

*June 23: Raining. A surprise! We didn't expect him on such an ugly
day. I am in the shower and come out just as he climbs the
stairs. I run with the towel trailing. He yells to George that
Helen is streaking. A real devil, he is! What slowly starts out as a
hand pose ends up in full posing position. He goes into a frenzy
full throttle! Water and paint splash, utensils fall, table tilts and
the painting becomes awash in splattering from all directions.
He talks to no one in particular. "You're beautiful." I'm almost
crazy, but not quite." I stay quiet and leave him in his frenzied
world of art. Some of it seems so careless, clumsy or destructive
but the end result seems to be his desire. He reminds me that I
am seeing the "real man" as strange as he seems.*

Andy continued to work on the painting through the end of the month,
enjoying respites in the pool. "Somehow, he must try out all the pleasures of
this house, which continues to amaze him," Helen noted.

*June 29: I doze briefly while he is distracted and wake, startled to
see him staring down at me through his horn-rimmed glasses,
ready to catch an unusual pose. I chastise him for intruding
and scaring me. We laugh a lot. He writes a note giving me
the painting if anything happens to him. I want you to know
I'm "real," meaning he keeps his promises. I choke up because
it's like a final goodbye. A very deep discussion, very sad and
difficult to talk about it. I choke now even while writing. God,
is he dramatic, compassionate and sensitive! He loves this place.
I think he is afraid he won't live long enough to fully enjoy it.
Sad. Father time hovers.*

*June 30: He shows up to view the painting then takes a walk in
the park (Brandywine Battlefield Park). He and I sit under a
poplar tree and wait for Lafayette's Headquarters to open. He
loves to reminisce about history, the area, people, etc.*

As Andy was about to make his annual summer trip to Maine, Helen
noticed sadness in the great artist. "He has himself all wrapped up in me as a
model and now must abruptly leave," she noted.

> *July 2: I ask if he doesn't get bored with one subject. He says there are
> so many facets to me that painting is exciting. He also feels the
> urgency because of his age. We sit on a bench on a side porch.
> He just looks at me and I see the sadness. We have become each
> other's confidante.*
>
> *July 3: Gone! I miss him. We (George and Helen) both miss him. He
> is on our minds constantly. He is a sensitive, passionate, intense
> on one hand, light on the other, humorous man, just bursting
> with life. He lives in a fantasy world, considering himself a
> "spirit" like it will help him live now and forever. "I am in my
> paintings," he says, "and you can see me there in all my work."
> What a man, what a handsome, devilish man! I just love him.*

Helen kept track of Andy's phone calls during the next two months, 14 calls in all. "He jokes, teases and is happy to surprise us," she wrote. Andy was sick with lung issues after he fell from a boat. He didn't tell Betsy. Andy said Betsy tore down a shed he was painting and loaned his car to someone for a long period of time. "This all adds to the agony of staying in Maine. He is miserable," Helen noted. Andy said Maine was drying up for him and he wanted to come home to Chadds Ford. "Where are Helen & George?" he pleadingly asked.

During one of the conversations, Andy recommended that Helen read a book, The Last Station. Andy contended the book depicted the life he shared with Betsy. Helen agreed and reported she found the book depressing, sad and miserable.

As Andy became immersed in creating a new painting, the calls to Helen and George slowed.

> *October 14: Now he is back! We could tell by the unlocked back door
> that he was here. Later that night we found a note on our bed
> under my pillow: "The Spirit has returned."*
>
> *October 16: We have a long talk about his summer, the girl he
> painted and his absence. I guess we all did miss each other. We
> have serious talks and he's really home again.*
>
> *October 18: I dress in full modeling outfit for the final pose. He
> shortens the hair and changes the cheekbone. He's very happy
> with it now and reframes it. All done!*

*October 20: He comes for the painting. George and I help him hang
it at the School House. It's goodbye to an "old friend." I am so
proud of this one. Who will buy it? Where will it go? He showed
Jamie the painting. Jamie was astounded and partly shocked
with the sexiness of it. He loves the figure (legs) and felt I had
just woken up from a nap with sleep still in the eyes. We saw
Andy's other new painting, "Overflow." Nice but not exciting.
Mine overshadows it by far. Andy says I can rest for a while.*

One cold October day Helen found Andy hiding in a bed in Painter's Folly
with blankets on top of him. He gave little whistles as clues as to his location.
"A good joke on me!"

*October 24: I'm in a slight depression, which makes me down but not
too obvious. We go to the Concordville Inn for lunch. He is in a
full jean outfit, jacket with the American flag). What a contrast
we are, (me in office dress clothes). He is so crude in some ways.
He eats with his fingers, grabbing food in a homey fashion.
I shrink in my chair for fear people will recognize him and
stare, a fear out of protection for him. He, on the other hand, is
surprising loud as he mentions obvious details such as museum,
painting, posing, models and family names. Looking around,
I realize he isn't so shy after all. I think he almost wants to be
recognized. Could he actually be disappointed that he isn't?*

Coming Ashore elicited many different views. Andy told Helen he didn't
like the painting and Helen agreed, saying it was too posed, too set and unreal-
istic. In contrast, Jamie believed the painting of Helen was his father's best work
in some time. Helga thought it was her legs in the painting. Frolic and Jamie
were impressed with the "gams."

*October 26: Note: George's car breaks down. We're in a stressful
situation. The carriage house is not rented, a situation created
by George and not a good one. We discuss it and I break down
completely. My heart is racing, chest hurts and I start crying
convulsively. Both hands are tingling and going numb. I fear a*

stroke or heart attack. Trembling!

*I must get hold of myself! I'm carrying the full financial burden of
our home and even though we hurt he asks no questions, gives
no comfort, has no inkling of what or how I pay the bills. No
questions. The taxes are due in five days. I write all this because
with Andy we are incurring expenses and he prevents us from
selling. He promises payment for modeling and to fix up our
house outside as a gift. Little does he know of our situation!! He
might never give anything. He could be tight or stringing me
along. We would have moved three years ago. God help us all! If
we ever survive this the advantage would be great. I don't want
to move. I love my house!*

*October 29: He stops to tell us Betsy's review of the new painting.
She thinks "Masquerade" is befitting as a title. She sees me as
a dancer or in the theater. She gets this feeling with the long
fingers and position of the arm and hand that's it is a very
mysterious person in the painting. Andy thinks she has chosen
a good title. I think it's both fabulous and dangerous in its
connotation. Oh, well!*

For Halloween, Andy brought Helen and George a laughing Vincent Price
skull. He also invited the couple to Jamie's Halloween party. The invitation
included a witch drawing. They arrived at the party as Andy and Betsy were
leaving. "Nice party," Helen noted. "Scary! Live python snake, great costumes,
good hors d'oeuvres. George wouldn't go to the Mill to surprise them. Too shy.
We go home."

The day after Halloween Andy visited a cold Painter's Folly. He retrieved a
winter's coat from his car to keep warm. Helen was embarrassed that he needed
to do so.

*November 1: He asks me how I am. I say, I'm not going to lie. I feel
like my world is falling on me. I mention the car situation,
empty carriage house, our house, etc. He gets stern: "Let George
take care of that. That's his responsibility." He condemns me for
not being stronger and worrying about material things. "Use
the truck," he says. "Do you need money?" I'll give you 3 or 4*

> *paintings, go sell them! You need a car? I'll go buy you one!"*
> *Then he mimics my pleas through tears and we both burst out*
> *laughing. All through it I say, "You don't understand." And he*
> *truly doesn't. Senseless to explain. I'm feeling low but he sees*
> *only a happier side to it and he stays in a fun mood. I have just*
> *unloaded some very personal information on him. I regret it.*

Andy took Helen to lunch at Vincent's restaurant in West Chester and then rode with her as she completed errands. "He wants to meet my boss," Helen wrote. "I can't believe it. My office is in my boss's home and I take him. Andy meets him and his wife and they are overwhelmed. What a crazy day. I give Andy directions for getting back on the main street with only two turns and find out he got lost."

> *November 2: George was getting the car fixed and Andy shows up. I*
> *was happy to see him until he presented me with an envelope. I*
> *tearfully blasted him for misinterpreting me yesterday. I felt that*
> *as a friend he was rude, presumptuous and not sympathetic. I*
> *throw the envelope at him. How many people have tried to tap*
> *him over the years? Has he become hardened? He says the gift is*
> *for posing, for a new dress that was offered before and something*
> *he does for all models; something he would like to do often. I'm*
> *upset with the whole situation and he makes a special effort*
> *to appease me. I will never confide in him about my personal*
> *problems again and I don't want his money!*

Before departing, Andy gave the leftover studies from Masquerade to Helen and signed them. He told Helen to keep them in a vault. Later in the day, Andy returned with country singer Ray Kennedy. "Ray sang to his tape and tore the heartstrings and tears right out of us," Helen recorded. "So emotional, so romantic, so touching. He held nothing back and entertained us royally." The next day Kennedy dropped off a copy of the tape for Helen.

> *November 4: Andy brings Nicky Wyeth for a visit. We discuss my*
> *painting. Nicky likes the painting but not the title.*
> *November 5: Andy calls from the Mill and announces that Betsy has*

renamed the painting "Beauty Rest." They are anxious to hear my opinion. I have none but I have to think about it. "Beauty Rest" seems too sweet for me, not nearly as mysterious. Am I disappointed? A little but also relieved.

Andy skipped painting the next few days as his toe hurt. One day he arrived on crutches with his foot swollen. On November 11, Andy called Helen from a hospital room. Andy was afraid an infection was in the bone marrow. "I exchange stories with him and we laugh heartily. He feels better, I know," Helen noted. Andy was diagnosed with gout.

Helen ventured to the hospital to visit Andy.

November 13: He is lying in bed with a Naval Academy robe, reading Truman Capote. The toe and part of his foot are truly swollen. I stay about an hour. He said Betsy says she loves what she has done in the museum but Andy won't like it.

November 15: Andy is on crutches and he wants us to meet him at the museum at 10 am for the preview. We meet Andy's Tennessee agent, Frank Fowler. Andy leads us into the gallery where my painting was in full direct view. It looked super! So much more bold, vivid, large and impressive. I'm thrilled in a very humble way. Betsy has a painting of a black reclining woman, similar in pose, next to mine. Interesting! Another painting of a dried carcass of animal bones follows. Mysterious. Andy thinks she did this with some jealous overtones. "Coming Ashore" was next to "Painter's Folly." A nice connection. Betsy showed up in a lovely wool sweater jacket, jeans and a hat. Lovely. She gives me a light hug and I sense a certain "Hollywood" greeting (superficial). George disagrees with my analogy. I'm very aware that visitors are staring like Holsteins and follow our movements. It's both embarrassing and titillating! Quite a bonus for the lucky visitors: the king and queen of the Wyeths and a model. Frank Fowler is taking "Glass House" to Dick Epps, the buyer. A very pleasant fellow, Frank, and full of spirit. George and I leave and overhear Andy telling Frank what nice people we are. Frank concurs.

A Sunday visit turned into a breakfast and then posing session. The artistic sitting quickly became a "deep soul searching dialogue." The conversations continued.

November 17: I'm very unhappy with my life at this time but cannot discuss this with him completely. I tell him so. He is too far removed from average, common problems to appreciate my woes. He also does not want to hear the downside of my life. He depends on me to lift him up and keep him young physically and mentally. He has little tolerance for my negative, troubled thoughts. I don't think he would make a good listener for Betsy. He needs my laughter, joy and compassion to excel in his paintings … it invigorates and stimulates him. Maybe Helga is right … he is selfish. Today I'm down and struggle to pretend otherwise. A very unusual friend. I always have the feeling he doesn't understand me. Does he? If I say I'm feeling blue he won't even question why. Strange friend.

November 23: I tell him he is caught up in self-satisfaction and self-preservation. He definitely is not interested in my personal life. I'm very frank with him. We banter back and forth, both arguing and laughing. I am very candid with him. I chastise him on his listening ability and lack of sympathy as a friend. He answers, "There really isn't anything I don't like about you." He said Betsy hung my painting next to the painting of the black nude with the remark: "There, that'll fix her." Betsy sees the painting as extremely sexy, even in the face. My, a controversial painting!

November 27: We are able to do some soul talking, revealing our strengths and weaknesses, aspirations, religion, family, etc. He says he is most open and honest with me. I should be flattered but can't help but feel I am only one of many in the same situation with him. Somehow, he talks and reveals too much and I would be afraid he would break my privacy and confidentiality.

December 1: I am beginning to see him through different eyes and it is disappointing. George and I both think he is flattered by

the jealous attention of his models: each vying for his attention.
We think he throws "carrots" to keep them hanging on. He says
he financially supports Ann Cole, Seri and Helga. Really?? I'll
find out. He certainly knows his worth and strengths. This part
disappoints me. I'm getting to know the REAL Andy Wyeth!

Helen realized Andy disclosed some intimate conversations they shared with his son Nicky. The betrayal was discovered when Nicky teased Helen about aspects of *Beauty Rest.* The disclosure of the personal matters to Nicky bothered Helen. When Andy contacted Helen to discuss Nicky's remarks, Helen told him she didn't sleep that night, an exaggeration.

Andy began spending more time with George as Andy was sketching George for a Christmas present for Helen. The gift was to be a secret but George disclosed he was also a model for Andy. George couldn't keep a secret. As Andy was sketching, he commented that George looked like Picasso.

December 8: We have a serious talk (soul searching, I call it). I tell
him about my feelings about my painting; it's a project done by
both of us, a very special friendship and how I don't relish being
used as a prop with my friends while they visit the museum. He
listens intently and fills up with tears. "That's what I like about
you, you're such a lady. I hold you on a pedestal."
December 11: Today he is concerned about the pain in his left hand.
He is in severe pain but does not want anyone to know. He talks
about the "end" for him in painting and is both angry and
despondent with the idea. His thoughts are scattered and slow
in expressing. I feel he is agonizing about his future. And, oh the
pain!
December 14: I put on the black gown and he hits on the nun idea
(for a painting). A good day for him.
December 15: Andy said he'll call the painting "Nun of That." We
laugh and laugh. I'm to get an old-fashioned nun's habit. It will
show the religious and serious side of me. With the mention
of religion, Andy and I get into a serious discussion. Does he
believe in God? "No! Only if I can catch him in a trap," he says.
I tell him of my faith in God. He wishes I had that faith in

HIM. He is god and "why not," he says. "No one appreciates the earth as I do." So strange to hear him, an atheist, talk like that.

Helen contacted St. Agnes Church in West Chester about borrowing a nun's habit. After the habit arrived, Helen felt "eerie" when wearing the outfit. Helen wrote, "Andy is in awe as I transform myself into a nun. He becomes almost religious."

As discussions about the nun painting continued, Andy mentioned he intended to sell one of his painting and give the cash to Helen and George to repair the house. "I want to make you happy, not just small things but big, exciting things," he said. Helen was thrilled and called George and told him of Andy's promise.

December 29: He is really excited and envisions the nun in an "open field running from Catholicism." It moves me to tears. His thoughts are so deep and words so eloquent. He is excited and splotches paint everywhere, making me nervous. He wipes his brush on his English Bombardier jacket, which was new for Xmas. I'm excited myself. A couple came to see Andy last month from overseas and visited the area, including passing our house. The husband, an artist, was shocked that Andy could paint so much from so little. Andy found that amusing and very interesting. He's beginning to say I am converting him to Catholicism. I'm beginning to wonder. He says he'll go to church with me sometime.

Notes: Stan and Elsa Zukin (Helen's employer and wife) met Andy again. It makes it easier to miss work when they feel involved. It's such a pain to keep up with this diary. I can't remember everything and don't have time to write really good notes. Andy is happier every day. He is excited about the nun habit. There was no Xmas party for the Wyeths.

CHAPTER FOUR
1992

Andy Is on Cloud Nine

Andy spent part of New Year's Day sketching and talking with Helen about religion, his art and friends, especially the Kuerners. Helen believed Andy was becoming interested in religion and "seems to be changing his tune" on the issue.

> *January 3: This is a long working session. He comes in a frenzy. He couldn't sleep thinking about the painting. "I'm confining myself by staying in this room. This room isn't right. We need to be in the widow's walk. The windows have a cathedral look." I tell him he is working too hard. He says he is slowing down but I don't believe it.*
>
> *January 5: We have a good session. When we go upstairs Andy must rest on the third floor before going to the widow's walk. I tell him to rest on the bed. He looks exhausted. I take off his shoes and rub his feet. He enjoys it so much that I turn him over and rub his back. This is not like him. I'm concerned.*
>
> *January 7: Andy called. He has a cold! I knew it!!*
>
> *January 8: When I come home he is sitting on the front porch, relaxed in the sun with his eyes closed. He said it was too cold in the house.*

In turn, Helen fell ill. Posing for Andy was difficult but the sketching continued. Helen reported that Andy was kind and considerate during his visits. During one session, Andy had Helen holding a rosary in her hands. Helen wouldn't have added the rosary to the painting as she felt the rosary simplified the picture and curtailed a viewer's imagination. After working on the painting one day, Andy left a note, saying "Stopped in to see Sister Helen."

When Andy dropped off a framed sketch of the painting, both George and Helen were excited and disappointed. The couple hoped the sketch was unfinished.

After not seeing Andy for a few days, Helen and George left him a note, "Wherefore art thou O'Spirit?" George also left him a comical "Last Will and Testament." Andy called to say he was fine.

> *January 17: At 2:20 a.m. he blows the horn and I yell out the*
> *window. The moon has become bright and he is afraid of missing*
> *it. George runs to turn on all of the heating systems. We coax him*
> *to lie on our bed to keep warm until the widow's walk warms up.*
> *I put on the habit and stand in front of the window for about*
> *ten minutes and he hurries home. All THAT for ten minutes!!*

Helen received a letter dated January 19 from Sister Elaine Wheeler of DePaul Provincial House of Albany, N.Y. The letter stated, "Knowing Mr. Wyeth's reputation as an excellent artist, I agreed to lend the habit to him to use for artistic purposes. Sister Loretta assured me that what he had in mind was to create a mood of nostalgia to remain in people's memory."

> *January 19: Tonight he walks in with a news flash! Betsy said she*
> *got an anonymous phone call saying Andy was seen at the*
> *Concordville Inn (at an auction). Andy gave her the whole story,*
> *including his painting project of the nun's habits. George, Andy*
> *and I doubt some of the story.*
> *January 21: He is very excited. He really means business today. At*
> *11:45 a.m. we go down for tea and have a lovely chat about*
> *religion, repairing the house, nature, feelings and death. A*
> *heart-to-heart talk with both of us teary eyed at different times.*
> *What an emotional, earthy person … to see and hear him is*

> *quite an experience. Somehow, the upcoming hospital visit is weighing heavy on his mind. He wants to 'go' without knowing it – just drop dead – and his doctor says that's probably what will happen. The idea of making final plans for death abhors him. It's not a real need for a man of his stature.*
>
> *January 26: Snow. A lot of progress today. The painting of the sitting nun is coming alive with every brush stroke. A real miracle in progress. He is pushing hard because of the upcoming hospital visit. He says snow makes him crazy. I believe him. He came in bursting with energy, having spent the early morning on the side of the hill. He told Betsy at 5:30 not to look for him, as he would be totally wrapped up in catching the snow scenes before it melted. I have a new appreciation for the white stuff.*
>
> *January 27: We go for lunch. He orders vodka drinks with a twist of orange, which is unusual for him. I think he needs it for medicinal purposes. He's been coughing a lot with blood spots, also a lot of wheezing.*

Andy continued working on the nun's painting and he believed the painting had quality. "Yes, we can do something with this one!" Andy said. He temporarily framed the panting, saying a framed painting "gives him a better feel for the look."

> *January 28: His philosophy is "grab the chance while you have it." He's on cloud nine. We eat and giggle. This successful painting has put him in a tizzy. We open fortune cookies and the fortunes are unbelievable for us both. I saved them in our mementos. He has lots of dreams for the nun outfits.*
>
> *February 1: My, he's in a jolly good spirit today. He just finished another painting called "Telephone's Ringing." I suspect it is of Helga in the studio. He really is knocking them out. Again, I think it's in anticipation of the operation.*

Andy's operation on his left hand took place at Jefferson Hospital in Philadelphia on February 5. The next day he alerted Helen that the operation was successful.

*February 8: He is in fine spirits! We laugh and joke. We gave him a
fake bloody finger. I pose standing with the small habit from
West Chester. The sitting nun is finished.*

*February 9: He finishes the watercolor of the standing frontal nun.
He compares painting to fencing … jabbing, darting, choosing
the good spots, good angles and hit and miss. I mention a few
major strokes of importance and he flips out with excitement.
"You're just like Betsy! How could I meet two women alike?"*

*February 10: He is anxious to report Betsy's response to the paintings.
She loves "Mother Superior." She finds her almost frightening,
strong and intimidating. She loves the feet on the sitting nun
("After Vespers"). Andy thinks it is too pleasant and rather
pretty to suit Betsy. She is jealous. George and I are afraid she
is dictating titles and opinions that will hurt the placement and
future of my paintings. I certainly feel the squeeze! She knows
nothing of me as friend or foe. Betsy also saw me in the Mother
Superior painting as domineering, being a good mother but
keeping the children at length. A rather negative connotation, I
thought.*

Andy continued his almost daily visits for the rest of the month even
though his hand was swollen and infected. One night he picked out some of the
stitches with his teeth.

*February 23: I went to the Baptist church. In walks Andy and George
and sit in the back seats behind me in church. They had decided
to surprise me. What a shock!! Andy left a banana skin on the
seat of the church. He had forgotten his hearing aid and had to
read the sermon pamphlet in anger to know what the sermon
was about.*

*February 24: George and I meet Andy and Frank Fowler. Frank
tours the widow's walk. I like Frank. He is unpretentious, fun,
interesting and probably loyal and honest.*

February 27: He called the office to say he would be at the hospital.

*February 29: Andy got a lot done on the nun close-up. My,
how sloppy he is while painting. Pools of watercolors run*

*uncontrolled over the painting. I'm so afraid to call his attention
to the splattering but it is frustrating*

*March 1: He is wearing an apron now, something he should have
done long ago. Is it because we have made him aware of the
paint on his clothes or is it Betsy after him for ruining his
sweaters? He does make a special effort to come looking good. I
think we keep him young. He mentions that Betsy will have him
buried in Maine with her family. I know he isn't happy with the
decision.*

*March 4: Andy brought 6 photographs of the nun paintings to share
with the nuns.*

Andy helped Helen and George fund the repairs on the house. Helen
recorded that Andy did other kindnesses.

*March 8: He is a very compassionate man and I asked him how
many people know the REAL ANDY. He responded, "None."
How sad. He is easily moved to tears and I respect him for that.
I am so used to hard, calloused men. He is touched when his
paintings stir emotions.*

The nun painting continued to be Andy's focus. He changed the background
to very dark that gave the rendering a bolder effect.

*March 14: He scrapes off part of the painting to uplift the corner
of the hat. First he wet it, then sanded. The paper peeled up
and I was afraid to watch him. He seemed to be ruining it. I
considered it potentially disastrous. But he seemed unconcerned.
He splashes paint everywhere, on the bed, floor and rug. I
fear that the habit will also get paint covered. Somehow, this
painting does not excite me.*

*March 15: He brought an empty frame and placed the finished
painting in it. I'm personally a little disappointed with the
habit's white bib. He has placed too dark of a blue line down
the front. He even brings this to my attention but doesn't quite
correct it. Oh well! He's the master. We have a lovely discussion*

when he finishes working. Why do I doubt him on so many little
remarks? We appreciate each other, our similar backgrounds,
families, interests and laugh a lot about each other's stories. I
love these moments.

March 18: He sharpens the chin and neck. Very subtle changes but
definite and important. It has feeling and strength. This work
is very tedious. Very little paint but a lot of brushing, which is
called dry brushing.

After the nun painting was completed, Helen noticed Andy had no new poses in mind for her. Helen also noted that Andy was following a familiar pattern. He seemed to be floundering without a project. Andy's health was also a concern. He was congested and admitted to spitting up dark mucous. Helga contended the maladies were caused by an infection from Andy's hand.

March 23, He puts finishing touches on the big picture (the nun close-
up). Each little stroke creates flesh and tone. He finally signs it,
packs it back in the frame and takes it home with him.

March 24: Betsy has called the new painting "The Mad Hatter" or
"The Broken Wing." I express shock and bewilderment. "Is this
to convey a comedy?" I ask. Andy says Betsy, Mary Landa and
Frolic love it the most. A real winner! Andy is proud and says,
"We pulled it off; we did it!" He is nice enough to include me.
He says he'll give me a break from posing. He says ideas are still
stirring his head.

March 25: Frolic chided Betsy for "Mad Hatter" as sacrilegious.
George and I suggest using the name of the hat "Coronet."
George calls Betsy as a ploy to introduce the new title. She fell
for it. George, Andy and I roar with laughter. Andy told Betsy
that we had to sell a property to fix the house. She suggested that
we be given paintings to sell for a commission and be an agent
for them. I can't believe it! Is Betsy being charitable? It would
help us with expenses.

March 31: Andy called to say his sister Ann was so impressed with the
painting "Coronet" that she wrote a piano composition for it.
The face totally inspired her.

Helen recounted a visit with Andy, Betsy and George at the Mill to see Betsy's just purchased antique pool table. George played a game with Betsy and Betsy was caught up in the excitement of the visit. Helen noted Betsy was friendly but naturally reserved.

> *April 7: He came early and we are barely out of bed. He comes up to the bedroom and we're in pajamas. Betsy would kill him if she knew he got us up!*
>
> *April 11: He shows up jaunty and full of vitality. We go to the widow's walk to visit. Great views and new roof looks good. He doesn't stay. I think he is just pacifying me by touching base. He looks great … tan, blue jeans and turtleneck. His capped teeth, slim body and composure somehow remind me of "upper crust." I am reminded, oddly enough today, that he truly is Andrew Wyeth. In reminiscing about a meeting he had with (a woman), he showed her around Chadds Ford and gave a sneak preview of the Helga paintings. He asked her if she would pose naked in a similar situation. She had written about it in a diary. Betsy and I both call him devious. He laughs at his own mischievousness. I see right through him.*

During the Easter season, Andy and Helen and George exchanged gifts. George dressed as an Easter bunny and carried a pot of tulips and a carrot to see Andy and Betsy. After Easter, Andy became inspired about a new painting, a few nuns sitting on a bench facing the house. George and Helen believed Andy's idea came from Helen Valloti liking the previous nun painting. Helen also saw Andy painting outside Painter's Folly. Andy said his painting was to be a "surprise."

> *April 30: He says he will retrieve one of his paintings and give it to us to sell. If anything happens to him we are to keep it. It is untitled but Andy thinks "Ring Farm" might be good.*
>
> *May 3: Betsy invited our family to the Mill to see the 3 nun paintings before they are shipped out of state. I heard "Mother Superior" and "Sister Helen" several times.*
>
> *May 5: He dropped off the paintings of the nuns for us. He told us*

*we could show them. He stayed only a short time as the family
was down to see Jamie as he went to the hospital to have stitches
removed from his arm.*

Four nuns of the Daughters of Charity arrived at Painter's Folly to see the paintings. Helen noted a "lively time" was had by all.

*May 13: He is troubled. Betsy and he are arguing. She wants him to
go to Maine early this year. He is going through the same yearly
scenario. He is tired of the "power" scene and just wants "peace."
Sad!*

*May 19: I put on the large nun outfit and we go to Kuerner's field.
It was beautiful! The field was covered with buttercups and
farm grass. We could see my house, the church and Lafayette's
headquarters nestled among the trees. Andy sat behind me to
paint. I found myself caught up in the emotion of it all. It was
so much like my old family home. I soon found tears running
down my cheeks.*

Helen's work in West Chester caused her to miss opportunities for other such pleasant outings. Andy wanted her to quit work and suggested putting Helen on his payroll. Helen didn't believe Betsy would allow her to do so.

During May, Andy spent time with his sister *Henriette. Andy was also interested in a trip to Cape May, NJ.*

*June 2: He stops in briefly. I'm going to the hospital for blood tests for
an upcoming surgery.*

June 3: Andy calls George to check on me. How nice of him!

*June 4: He went to Cape May yesterday. He eventually fesses up but
doesn't say who with. Says he went down for ideas for painting
me. Sure!?! He has brought up the idea of my quitting work
several times but I really don't know what's on his mind. I think
he is jealous of someone else controlling me when he can afford
to buy me out and have me around for posing. Time will tell.*

*June 6: It's the 25th anniversary at the museum. Terribly exciting. I
wore a beaded silver and black formal dress. Smashing! George*

was in a tux. Andy danced with me. He wore a terribly heavy winter's tux. He is not a good dancer but thinks he is. Helga was with him but he said her husband was there. A lie! He was embarrassed bringing her as a date. He didn't expect us to be there. Getting me to dance with him was throwing me a "bone" as far as I'm concerned.

June 7: Andy and Nicky stop in. Andy studies me carefully for a reaction to last night. They didn't stay long.

June 8: Andy called to ask about me. I had two small spots removed from my right breast.

June 9: The three of us go to the Daughters of Charity in Wilmington for dinner. There were 7 nuns. In conversation Andy asked the sisters how many believed in abortion. I thought I would choke!

June 10: Andy exchanges the sitting nun paintings. He leaves us his "study" to sell.

June 14: Andy and I are working on the third floor. George taps on the door and surprises us with the nun outfit on again. An unusual sight! Should have had a picture of George!

June 15: Andy stayed overnight to be ready the next morning for Cape May.

June 16: The three of us eat breakfast along the way. Andy heads straight for the life boat and we pose and paint. I wear the full habit. Eventually I take a break and fall asleep. I awake to find him painting my feet and sleeping body. The rascal! We drive to St. Joseph's Convent. I still have the habit on. We ask permission to cross their property. The word quickly spreads and people are 'casually' appearing on the balconies and in lawn chairs. The ask us in. They had lined up like a reception in the kitchen area.

Andy wasn't through with the nun's habit. He once again asked Helen to pose in the outfit before the clothing was returned.

Before departing for Maine, Andy reminded Helen that he was only a "Spirit."

June 19: As we pass through the kitchen he tells me to look the other way. He kisses the back of my neck and deliberately keeps walking. He drops his hands hard as I speak indicating that he found it hard to say goodbye. He never looked back. I managed to grab his jacket sleeve, gave him a fast peck and said, "I'll see you in the fall." And then he was gone.

Note: How do I feel with his leaving? Mixed emotions! I can't rest until I know he is out of the area. There is creeping sadness and loneliness. Monday relief! Blessed relief!! No more shopping for Wyeth emergencies. No more surprise visits. No more morning teas and snacks. No more lies or half-truths. How does George feel about his parting? He misses him right away but is enjoying relief. We knew we would be going to Maine this summer.

Andy invited Helen and George to spend time with him and the couple arrived on September 8. That evening the Sipalas dined with Betsy and Andy. The next day Helen and George visited many of the Wyeth sites in Maine. Additional touring, visiting and dining took place. During the last dinner, Helen recorded a nasty scene.

September 15: Betsy started picking her female guest apart. I can't believe her cunning, deceitful, manipulative, power play in her stories. Suddenly, without provocation, she twists the story and places me in it. She blasts Andy and me. Betsy's true personal feelings were erupting through a split personality. She ranted and raged at Andy. Her face contorted and she paced the floor in anger. It was accelerating into a nasty situation. When we gently and pleadingly protested she got even angrier. Andy, to my surprise, started taking the blame and crumbled like tissue. "As a child everything was always my fault and I've always just taken the blame. I'll do that now, it's all my fault," he said. So pathetic. "I think the evening has ended," he said and rose from his chair. Betsy hugged George, kissed him and squeezing him tightly while facing me, and raved about what a good man he is. We left in shock and disbelief! Now, do we really know Betsy? How many people have encountered this side of Betsy?

The next night Betsy called to make sure they returned safely home to

Painter's Folly. She ended the phone call with "love you." Two days later Andy called and commented that Betsy had acted "like a crazy woman after we left that night."

> *Note: Andy clears the table, does dishes and is expected to serve. He is very subservient around her. She reins with an iron hand. Money or no money, Betsy could never be my personal friend! Too calculating and cold. Andy through Betsy finally found a friend (me) while we were in Maine. She warmed up considerably after getting to know me. Andy thought Betsy wanted to outdo me with cooking and entertaining. Jealousy? Truly, she is jealous. Her affection for George is exaggerated. All these were Andy's thoughts and/or facts expressed on the phone after we left Maine.*

Helen and George learned Andy had returned from Maine in October. The three of them had breakfast with Nicky at Hank's. As they departed, Helga arrived and they all went back to Painter's Folly. Helga played the organ poorly and too loud. Helga spied Andy's paintings of Helen and sunk into a sullen mood. "A very strange possessive person," Helen wrote.

> *October 20: This was a bad time. We discuss the whole Maine visit and rehash Betsy's episode. Things have changed this time. The talk is heavy and the subject of religion is deep. How or will he ever understand a person's faith. He truly thinks he can replace God and is disappointed when he sees he can't. Oh how he tries to get me to give it up. It's something he can't compete with and he admits it. I think he's used to total adulation. Here is a strong combination of fame, fortune and atheism. Sad, very sad.*
>
> *Evening: George and I check the third floor. He has taken everything of his work. Not one sketch is left! Motive? Not really sure. He didn't win with me? My gut feeling is he's not coming back real soon.*
>
> *October 21: I call him at the studio. He's feeling blue.*
>
> *October 22: I see him on Kuerner's hill. There is lots to talk about. The conversation is depressing.*

October 25: Andy called. He is in bed with a lung congestion. Helga
gave him a shot. He had a fever.
October 26: Andy shows up. He's feeling better.

Helen doesn't record any visits by Andy during Halloween.

November 1: Here he is again. I really missed the man and he
is excited to be here. A lot of catching up to do with the
news. George, Andy and I have tea and leave for church. It's
communion Sunday, a first for George and Andy. "Betsy would
be more shocked than if I went to a whore house," laughs Andy.
Note: Betsy has renewed her furor over the Helga paintings since
returning from Maine. This has made things rough (for Andy)
at home. She is still hurt and angry and the Helga exhibition
renews the pain. She tells Andy not to paint any more nun
material.
November 11: Andy surprises us in bed. He stretches out on the bed
with us, perfectly normal. He is excited about our party. Betsy
wants us to invite OUR friends. He also names Karl Kuerner.
Now, I'm really excited!

Andy contends he reclaimed all of his paintings from Painter's Folly because of pending sales. Helen doesn't believe Andy's explanation. "A very strange feeling," Helen wrote. "He seems to have purposely cleaned house. I don't pose anymore. I have strong mixed emotions. I miss him. Is this a strategy, punitive or just losing interest here? I think Betsy might be cutting a wound. After all, Nicky says she kills all his friends. It is strange how he is so possessed by her. George is the same way as Betsy."

November 19: Andy surprised George in bed. I am in the shower
and he knocks on the door. I won't open it. I find him under the
bedspread with all his heavy clothing on. I jump on the bed and
cover him from head to toe. We all can be so silly. He laughs so
much, no wonder he likes coming.
November 25: He is at the house. I wonder what he really does in
my house! Snoop?? I really don't trust him. He will, by his own

> *admission, take something if he wants it. A little disturbing.*
>
> *November 28: George and I left early for a Xmas tree. Andy returned as we placed the tree in the family room. We put the tree in a bucket and filled it with water until a hole was discovered in the bucket. Andy got a big kick out of the commotion. The posing was a real inconvenience but the master calls!*
>
> *December 10: Andy asks me to lunch but I can't. He says he hears "too many nos, I'll go ask Helga." I'm a little bothered and then get enraged as the morning progresses. I'm trying to make a living. Helga's at his doorstep seven days a week. I felt it was a put down!*

The Christmas party for the Wyeths took place on December 12 with a number of guests and an accordion player for entertainment. Helen's friends were shocked at being invited to a party with the Wyeths. The party was a success, Helen wrote. In the days before Christmas, the Wyeths and the Sipalas exchanged visits and gifts. Andy visited but did no more painting.

CHAPTER FIVE
1993

N. C. Wyeth Was an Excellent Critic

Andy began the New Year with a morning visit to Helen, who was resting in bed listening to classical music. They spent two hours visiting and sharing stories. George understood Andy needing "therapy" or venting time with her, according to Helen. A few days later, Andy was again venting, relaying a disagreement he had with Betsy. Andy asked Betsy, "Why can't we be like the Sipalas?" Betsy countered, "Why can't you be like George?"

Andy continued to visit the Sipalas' house when the couple wasn't home. Helen continued to be concerned about Andy's activities in her home when she wasn't there.

January 19: Privately, I'm still bothered by who's in the house while
we're away. George and I go to the preview at the museum.
George was ahead but returned quickly to say I'll be shocked
when I see the Wyeth show! A new nude picture ("Lady in
Waiting") is next to Widow's Walk. It is a woman in the
window of the third floor behind the shutters. I am more than
SHOCKED! There was a woman in my house and I didn't even
know it. So, this is the reason for the secrecy. The shock, and, yes,
anger eats at me all week. Why didn't he warn me? The painting
is sloppy and the face ugly. It doesn't fit in with my house. I feel
violated, like someone burglarized the place. Did she roam the

house; look in rooms, nosey around? This isn't right. George doesn't agree.

January 20: We leave in his car for Cuisine's Restaurant. I'm upset with him regarding the show and can hardly contain myself. I finally tell him I did go to the show but still refuse to mention the incident or my feelings. I didn't enjoy the lunch or his company.

January 28: Andy comes while I'm in the shower. George and he get under the covers and call me for the phone. I run to the room in my blouse and panties and they surprise me. A really good joke. Where could Andy have as much fun?

January 30: He comes with his pad and pencils. He is determined to start sketching me again. I believe him. I mention only briefly that I would be offended if he brought women in my house and I quickly gave him some thoughts on the "Lady in Waiting." He was surprised and concerned by my brief thoughts and feelings.

January 31: He's back! Andy and I retreat to the third floor for posing. It looks like he is serious again. I bring him up to date on the museum story and the turmoil it created. He is apologetic and is eager to make amends. Initially, he tried to lie. He explains that it is a sketch of our house, (two different people for face and body). Little does he know how obvious the fabrications are. It's just a way of life with him. I would not want to be Betsy! You can't trust him.

Andy suffered from the flu, as did Helen and George and sketching sessions ceased. Sketching and conversations continued after they recovered. One of the discussions centered on the singer Michael Jackson. Jackson once visited Andy and Andy considered doing a painting of Jackson.

February 16: Snow. Somehow, we all know where we stand with each other and feel comfortable. He doesn't have to win us over, impress us, and we are more relaxed.

February 21: Andy and I had a nice chat. I told him of my daydreams about him. I said I see him as a thief, pulling very personal information from his models, painting them on canvas

*and then floating them around the world for people to judge
and enjoy. I also see him as a knight on a horse, running over
the hills, the lance as energy and talent. Again, I see him as a
liar. Fame makes him so by forcing him to hide for privacy. He
is intrigued and amused. His real dream was of Michael Jackson
on Kuerner's hill. Andy in his French uniform and Jackson in
his braided one. Michael was dancing for him.*

*March 1: We were getting concerned as we hadn't seen him since last
Monday. He saw George and then called me to say he had been
sick again. He was spitting up blood from his lungs.*

*March 2: He rushes up with a new painting idea. He wants us in bed
with just the tops of our heads showing. He is very excited.*

*March 4: He gets George and I back in bed to pose. He works very
quickly and the idea materializes. A great idea. He dismisses
George and spends time sketching me. He looks to be his old self
today, laughing, spry, silly and fun! In our talk he mentioned
his problems with Betsy again. She made a list of everything she
didn't like about him last week. He reminded her that Jane did
the same thing to Nicky. He's almost embarrassed to discuss it
with me.*

*March 7: He told me the story of having dinner with Susan Miller
at the Squire. The waiter served something Andy didn't like and
he threw it on the floor. Strangely, he was proud and thought it
proved his manhood. "You thought I was a cream puff, right?"
I didn't hide my shock and scolded him for such behavior. He
howled about the whole thing but I do believe I left him with a
bit of shame.*

The next few days Andy sketched Helen and George. The work was
interrupted by a March blizzard.

*March 30: He came upstairs with a pad but didn't sketch. I don't like
being taken for granted. I never know when he's coming or if
he'll even paint when he gets here. So many times the sketchpad
is just a pretext for talking or unloading. I'm honored and
annoyed at the same time.*

April 4: He gave up on the painting of George and me in bed. It's too much "sleeping beauty." Before leaving, he looks for a painting he has hidden of George and me. It's great and I rejoice with it. I admonish him for dropping the idea and, as a result, renew his interest with a vengeance! He said he wants to do me nude on a bed when warmer weather comes. I refuse. I don't have the body for it and I don't think he's serious enough. I won't do it!

April 5: Andy sneaks in our bedroom and scares me to death. I scream instinctively. That scares George. Immediately George and I pose under the covers. Andy is excited. He finishes a sketch and might do a tempera. After I finish posing he flops across the bed and we get into deep discussions. It was very relaxing for him! Andy says he is "honored" by entering our private rooms and sharing his thoughts with me. Ann Cole said Andy will die within this year. We are all horrified! How crass of her!

April 8: Another surprise visit. He and Betsy have been fighting again. It's all about Helga again. She can't see why Andy didn't paint her instead of Helga. He mentions giving up painting.

April 10: Heavy rain. We dress for dinner and I put the Easter mask and white jumpsuit on and George wears a Perot mask with his dinner clothes. We stop in at the Wyeths and surprise them. The river is over-flowing and a glorious sight! Their reception is warm, cordial and friendly. The sight of the Brandywine (river) was awesome. Their doors were open for viewing. The water was relatively calm, not angry. Most everything was under water except their drive.

April 13: He officially started the tempera. He broke an egg, drained the yolk and membrane separately and mixed it with distilled water. Here we go on a new experience. Fun! He said he is taking ginseng, an aphrodisiac, along with Jamie for sexual stimulation. I think it's silly and ridiculous and I tell him so. Why is he so obsessed with sex at his age (76)? George and I aren't like that. I can see that paint is going to be everywhere!

April 15: He is deep into the tempera and working like a beaver. He works hard and rests two or three times, falling across the bed. How casual he is and how comfortable. The painting is taking on various moods and colors … some pleasant and some questionable.

Andy continued to work on the painting until 2:00 p.m. every day. When alone, he answered the phone, "Sipolas' butler." He had trouble pronouncing Sipala and to the end always added an "o" to their name. Andy gave Betsy updates on the painting and she was thrilled. "They're wonderful people, aren't they?" Betsy asked. Andy, George and Helen were all amazed, pleased and surprised at Betsy's support of the painting.

Helen spent hours posing and found it difficult to keep up with her employment and work around the house. Her back and neck hurt and she wrote her nerves were shot. "Posing is hard and so is the work of the artist," she wrote. Andy worked most days and George brought him fruit, cheese and crackers.

April 21: I surprise him at noon. He is eager to share his work with me. He said he just "loves it here. I'm excited with what I'm doing." He is on a new high … totally absorbed in the painting. I've never seen him so happy. All is well with Betsy and she knows where he is. The panting is dramatically progressing. He is totally upbeat! His interpretation of the star in the painting reduced me to tears. His urgency in life is intense. Death is a definite threat.

April 23: He works alone all day. Progress is slow but strong.

April 24: He arrives at 5:44 a.m. We are expecting him. He is eager to see the sun rise in our bedroom.

April 25: He's working us hard since our weekends are free

April 27: He told me that when he sells this painting he is going to give me a big chunk. He feels sorry for me having to work and doesn't like Stan taking advantage of me.

April 29: He is so excited about the progress of the painting. This is the first time he ever painted a tempera on his lap instead of an easel. He's delighted. He's cold. He finally starts to warm up. He thinks he is dying. "Maybe I'll die next week, tomorrow, maybe in a half hour."

May Day gifts were exchanged between Helen and George and Andy and

Betsy. Helen's garden grew as Andy gave her flowers. She planted them near flowers that were previous gifts from Andy.

Andy returned to painting and George did some creating of his own. George invested time with his camera in capturing Andy creating.

May 2: I went to church and came back to see Andy and George on the porch with their tongues hanging out waiting for lunch. A silly sight! Andy can't sleep at night deciding on the correct frame. It's nearing completion now.

May 3: He brought the frame, a light gray rough panel type. George helps him nail it together. He takes the painting and frame home, as Betsy is anxious to see it. She calls George and says she loves it. The name is to be "Dawn." Perfect!

May 7: Sunny and nice. He works alone. It was sort of fun having him around. He meets with Helen Valotti at 2 p.m. She has prints to be signed. He refuses. "My signature won't be worth 15 cents," he complains. "You're selling them too cheap and too many." She denies flooding the market. The frame is all wrong; too light and distracts from the painting.

May 8: Helga drives up and parks. She slowly drives away, stopping every 15 feet. She really wants to come in but can't quite bring herself to do so. We lock the doors and hide from her. Andy doesn't want her here. He's too busy. Sad girl! We invite Bell and Ed Granite to see the painting. "I want to pull back the covers and climb in too," says Ed. "I wish I could afford to buy it. Wouldn't it be nice to have your neighbors asleep on your wall?"

May 9: At one point he hands me the brush and tells me to do a little painting. He handed George the brush with the same instructions. We both objected, claiming we weren't artists and would ruin the painting. He insisted. We both added a stroke or two, making us part of the painting. We did this for posterity. George and I both signed the back of the painting.

The painting received rave reviews from friends and family. Frolic Weymouth was excited about the painting and Andy's sister Ann welled-up with tears upon seeing it. Betsy, Frolic and Andy all lauded the models, George and Helen.

May 13: He is so jubilant with the feedback and the results of his work. I can't get over how spirited he is, how youthful! He tells George to get a camera for funny bed photos. Helga came up the drive again but didn't come in.

May 14: My bed excites him in a strange way. I think he fantasizes about George and me. He wants to do a painting of George and me in a naked clutch. That's too erotic for me. I won't do it but George would. I won't be part of it. Kinky!! Andy swears that it's not if it's done well.

May 15: Wyeths' anniversary. Our bed pictures didn't turn out good. We take some more. The joke bed scenes are dangerous and we know it. Anything done in innocent comedy in the bedroom could be tainted for a man of his reputation, as innocent as it is. Today's discussion was depressing and sad. We spoke of death and he envisions just "disappearing" someday. He reassures me again that he will always be with me in spirit. He drives me to tears.

May 16: I told Andy a peaceful soul depends on a relationship with God. At the mention of God he stays quiet. I tell him the story of my mother's grave, birds singing and possibly a message from my mother. I choke up. He's fascinated and compassionate. Such a tender person he is. He has these cold spells: freezing when it's warm outside (80 degrees.) We force him under the covers His body is older and fragile.

May 20: Betsy has renamed the painting "Marriage." It's ok with me but "Dawn" had a better and softer sound. I reprimand Andy for being depressed. He said, "But you must allow me that. I'm always thinking of sad things, like soldiers in the battlefield, history, family. It's ok."

May 21: I ask Andy who he would choose to critique this painting. He thought for a moment and said his father. Andy said he was an excellent critic. "He gave the most honest, simple answers and reasoning to art problems. My father asked Peter Hurd to teach him the tempera method. Hurd's knees were wobbling and he compared the challenge to telling an admiral how to fight a war. Frightening." He said he is not interested in possessions. "I have

> *money and I don't even care. Betsy could tell you." He hit me*
> *with the idea of posing with George in a sexual embrace again.*
> *I refuse! No redeeming value to something similar to porno. I*
> *think it's just erotic and would not amount to anything except a*
> *turn-on for Andy. Andy said he did a painting with Seri and a*
> *foreigner with dark skin and it is in a vault in Kennett Square.*
> *True? Maybe! He said a whole series could be done on George,*
> *me and the house.*
>
> *May 22: Andy says Betsy finds George exciting and thinks he might*
> *have a problem because of his height. She finds him attractive in*
> *a sensuous way. She also thinks there is electricity in the painting*
> *similar to" Christina's World." She sees George as a horseman, so*
> *to speak, a perfectionist and me as an unbridled thoroughbred.*
> *Andy sees me in the movie Pygmalion, as almost a rags to riches*
> *person. He leaves the table, came to give me a kiss, shook George's*
> *hand and headed for the car. We wave as he pulls out. This whole*
> *day seems like a farewell. I'll bet we don't see him until he comes*
> *back from Maine. They leave the 24th. I feel absolutely confident*
> *that we are his closest friends at this time in his life.*

The time came for Andy's annual visit to Maine. Andy said he didn't want to go, as he did every year, but Betsy insisted the change in scenery was needed for both of them. "I get dragged away while I'm enjoying life and my work just because someone thinks I need a change," Helen quoted Andy as saying.

> *May 23: He's back again! He told us stories of his childhood. He*
> *couldn't read until he was 15 years old. He received a letter from*
> *Carolyn and couldn't read it. Peter Hurd asked him to look up*
> *something in the dictionary and found out Andy didn't know*
> *his alphabet. Peter taught him. Jamie got a doctorate at Bates*
> *College and in his speech told the students that they just wasted*
> *four years of their lives if they were going to be artists.*

Andy returned from Maine in June and visited Helen and George. "The three of us are jubilant! We give him a hearty warm welcome," Helen reported.

> *June 3: Epps doesn't want the painting ("Marriage"), too personal.*

Frank (Fowler) is very disappointed, of course. They aren't sophisticated enough for it, according to Frank and Andy. George showers and streaks through our bedroom with just three neckties tied strategically on his naked body. Andy and I are relaxing on our bed. Hilarious! Later I shower and modestly "streak" around the corner in my underwear. Andy falls apart with laughter. Helga follows Andy. She buzzes us on the intercom but Andy and I can't see her. She's in the house and we don't know it. Andy runs to the third floor and locks the door. She leaves before reaching the stairs. Expressing concern that Andy would be angry, she finally left. Andy has a talk with her (Helga), telling her to stay away from our house. He has to be firm with her because she is a strong-willed German."

June 4: Rain. I go to work. He works and sleeps all morning. He really wanted company today and teased that he might as well go back to Maine. I slip home for a half hour. I find him sleeping on my bed like it's his own. Oh, the privacy here is so delicious. He can hide from everyone including Helga, especially since she has taken over the studio. He loves it here.

June 7: He came into our bedroom. His coat pockets are full of sand and shells. He went to the beach yesterday with Carolyn Ryan. The sand pours out into my bed in a mound. Ugh! Betsy found out about Carolyn and Andy and was furious. Susan also found out and she was jealous. He tells all. I don't appreciate his Hollywood antics. I don't act bothered at all as I think he is looking for a reaction to his escapades. We're seeing little of him as he gallivants with Carolyn and Helga. If Betsy only knew! My opinion of him is changing. He swears the truth and lies like the devil. Let him enjoy himself. It will be short lived.

June 9. He stopped in. I'm cool with him and we all feel it.

Two days later Andy invited Helen and George to dinner at the Dilworthtown Inn with seven other people, including Helga. Helen recounted Helga is upset at the seating arrangement and pouted during the meal. "Andy spends the night babysitting her. Andy literally treats her like a child. The other guests ignore her."

> *Note: We see very little of him. George and I can't help but wonder*
> *where he is. I bought his favorite foods, expecting him for dinner*
> *occasionally. We feel tied up and inconvenienced not knowing*
> *if he is coming or going. It's easier when he is in Maine or when*
> *Betsy is home.*
>
> *June 15: We hear him come in (2 a.m.). He doesn't say where he was*
> *and I don't ask. I get thoroughly disgusted with him, as I can't*
> *stand the lies! But I don't offend him and hold my tongue. He*
> *takes the fun out of listening to him.*
>
> *June 17: He sneaks in the bedroom. "I created a monster," Andy says*
> *of Helga. "I can't and won't drop her; I'm too loyal." I think he*
> *really enjoys her company. He encouraged her to return to the*
> *Fraulein that she was: braids, peasant dress and her German*
> *heritage. "I changed the Olsens too," Andy said. "No one would*
> *go near their house. I've never told anyone before and you can*
> *tell after I'm gone that I washed Christina's face, hands, and feet*
> *and brushed her hair! She adored me. No one else ever cared*
> *before." Andy told a story about a Hollywood friend he took to*
> *the Olsen home. The man threw up and asked how Andy could*
> *stand the smell. "I never minded," Andy said. "I changed them,*
> *and I admit it. I'm a Jekyll and Hyde." I'm wondering how he*
> *changed me.*

For a time, Helen remained upset with Andy's antics. After one dinner, which induced Andy dancing with Helen, Helen wrote, "Why does he make me so sad? A fast answer is my disgust with his lies. We find ourselves shifting through his stories for the truth."

Several days later, Andy returned and stated he better return to Maine soon since his escapades were backfiring on him. Helen didn't record the antics or how the actions were causing Andy issues. Andy returned to Maine and he made periodic calls to Helen and George.

> *Note: Of all the women in his life, I would count (Helga) as #2 (Betsy*
> *being #1).*
>
> *Note #2: He promised to give George and me something for posing. I*
> *don't see that happening.*
>
> *July 8: He calls. We're both in a good mood. I'm not angry anymore*

and he thinks everything is just fine. He has disappointed me
with his antics and I have lost a lot of respect for him.
August 1: Andy's been sick with lung problems. He is getting better
with Dr. Valloti's care.
August 11: He's still a little sick. A very depressing call. He's homesick,
lonely, sick and very much down today. I can't cheer him up.
September 19: Andy called. He broke his wrist. He fell on the rocks
on the island.

When Andy did return to Chadds Ford, he called upon his good friends
Helen and George to give him a ride home from the Philadelphia airport.

October 7: We give Andy a wig to ride through Chadds Ford to
avoid everyone, especially Helga. We rode to my hometown,
Embreeville. Andy was touched by it all. I felt self-conscience
enjoying the ride around George. George doesn't understand these
surroundings like Andy and me. A lovely day and evening. There
was only one negative: we don't believe the broken wrist story.
October 9: I pose on the staircase but I won't disrobe for him. I
just can't take him serious all the time. He says I've lost my
"spontaneity." I don't care. He leaves in a bit of a huff.
October 16: He takes me to Carolyn's studio to pose. I tell him that
sometimes I can't stand the "magic" hand (his painting hand).
So many people, especially women, chase after him. The whole
thing makes me sick. He tells George and me that Helga went
to Eight Bells in Maine for a visit. Each time he tells the story
it is different. Again, he lies! My attitude is changing and he
scampers to pacify me.

One of the trips to Carolyn's studio was preceded by a visit to Jamie's home
and lunch.

October 16: When he speaks of my home place and my parent's grave
he literally cries. This has prompted him to paint the father/
daughter scene. He sensed I was introducing him to my parents,
which, indeed, I intended but felt sort of silly with George there.

> *Andy and I feel things differently. George would have laughed.*
> *We talk about my religion and he again says he is god. It is hard*
> *to believe this. An atheist. He wants to be my god! I pray for the*
> *right answers for such a lost man.*
>
> *October 24: He asks about my father's funeral. I suppose his*
> *intentions are honorable and sincere. He plans to show me*
> *standing and looking down over my father's casket. Weird but*
> *so much like Andy. We only work for half an hour and I stop for*
> *church. A disappointment and shock to him. I think he wants*
> *and expects me to make a choice: God or him. I choose God. I*
> *along with other models have put Andy first. He's getting spoiled*
> *and greedy.*
>
> *October 30: I'm edgy today. George and I suspect he is taking Helga*
> *to the Halloween party at the museum. I'm irritated just*
> *thinking about it. Jealousy? Certainly! He does so much for and*
> *with her. I'm sure Andy can't figure me out but our principles*
> *and lifestyle contrast sharply. I must retain my dignity even if*
> *he gives up. Betsy invites us to see the new Wyeth movie. Now,*
> *that's a real shock! We go, delighted of course. A fantastic and*
> *powerful movie! It makes George and I realize what a master,*
> *legend and person he is … something we've gotten used to.*

On Halloween, Andy began the day by attending church with Helen.

> *November 6: Andy brings Susan and Heide Miller over. I like Susan.*
> *She is the perfect replacement for Helga … young, plain, earthy*
> *and single. She "wants him," so Andy says, but I wonder for*
> *what reason. He thinks all models are jealous.*
>
> *November 16: At the end of the day we see a drawing of a casket and*
> *several people around it: Mrs. Kuerner, Betsy, Helga, Jimmy*
> *Lynch and me. It's Andy's funeral. We are shocked!*

George and Helen visited the Brandywine River Museum to see the *Marriage* painting. A guide mentioned to Helen, "I have a sneaky suspicion that this is Mr. & Mrs. Sipala at Painter's Folly. Why in the world would anyone want Mr. Wyeth to paint them in bed is a mystery to me!"   Helen burst out laughing. Later Helen shared the story with Andy and George called Betsy to replay the episode.

> *November 20: He explains the new picture idea. It's his funeral*
> *(taken from my father's funeral) with friends around the casket.*
> *He has a French uniform on and friends are coming down*
> *Kuerner's hill, making their paths like threads towards the*
> *casket. Perhaps Helga will be nude in the background "like she's*
> *a part of life but not accepted by Betsy." This idea is secret and*
> *all the work will be done in our house. We're thrilled.*
> *December 17: He throws $1,000 in $100 bills up in the air. At first*
> *he said it was for posing. Later he said he didn't know what to*
> *give me for Xmas so "buy yourself something."*

The Wyeth Christmas party was hosted on December 18. In the morning, Andy arrived with gifts from Betsy and him. A grand evening took place with delicious food and drink and a harpist, Mary Tooke. Andy declared the event a "mystical evening."

The money Andy gave Helen was used to pay part of the tax bill owed by the Sipalas. The spending on taxes upset Andy. "I thought you'd be running through Macy's shopping," Andy responded. Helen noted that Andy didn't realize the amount he gave her was not able to fully fund the tax bill.

> *December 23: He's wearing a long German fashioned military coat,*
> *olive with large buttons and reaching his ankles. It was made*
> *by Ralph Lauren. Weird! He loves it! Nicky gave it to him for*
> *Xmas.*
> *December 25: He brought us a bottle of homemade wine given to him*
> *by a friend. He wanted to thank us for our gifts.*

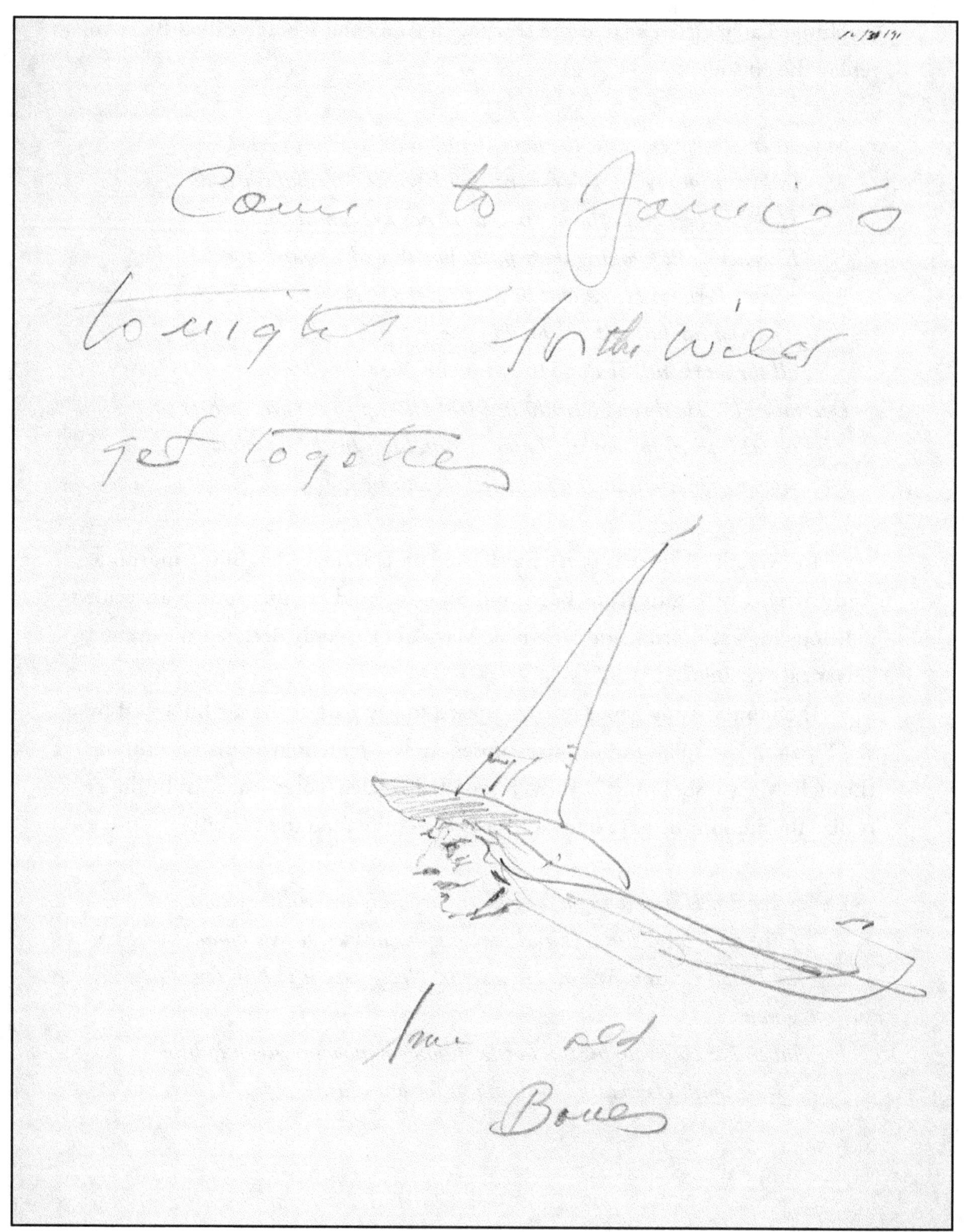

10/30/91   Invitation from "Old Bones"

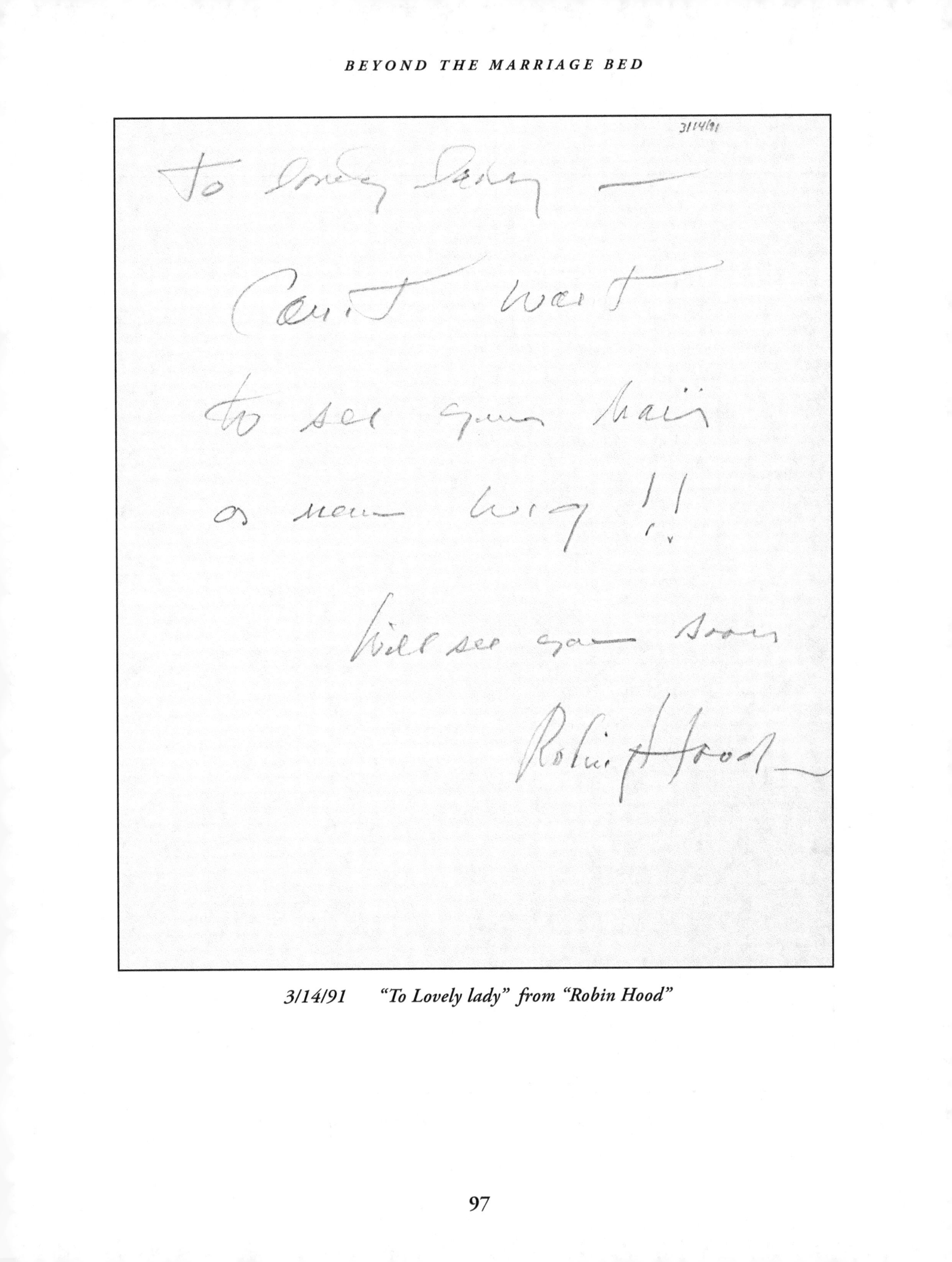

3/14/91   *"To Lovely lady" from "Robin Hood"*

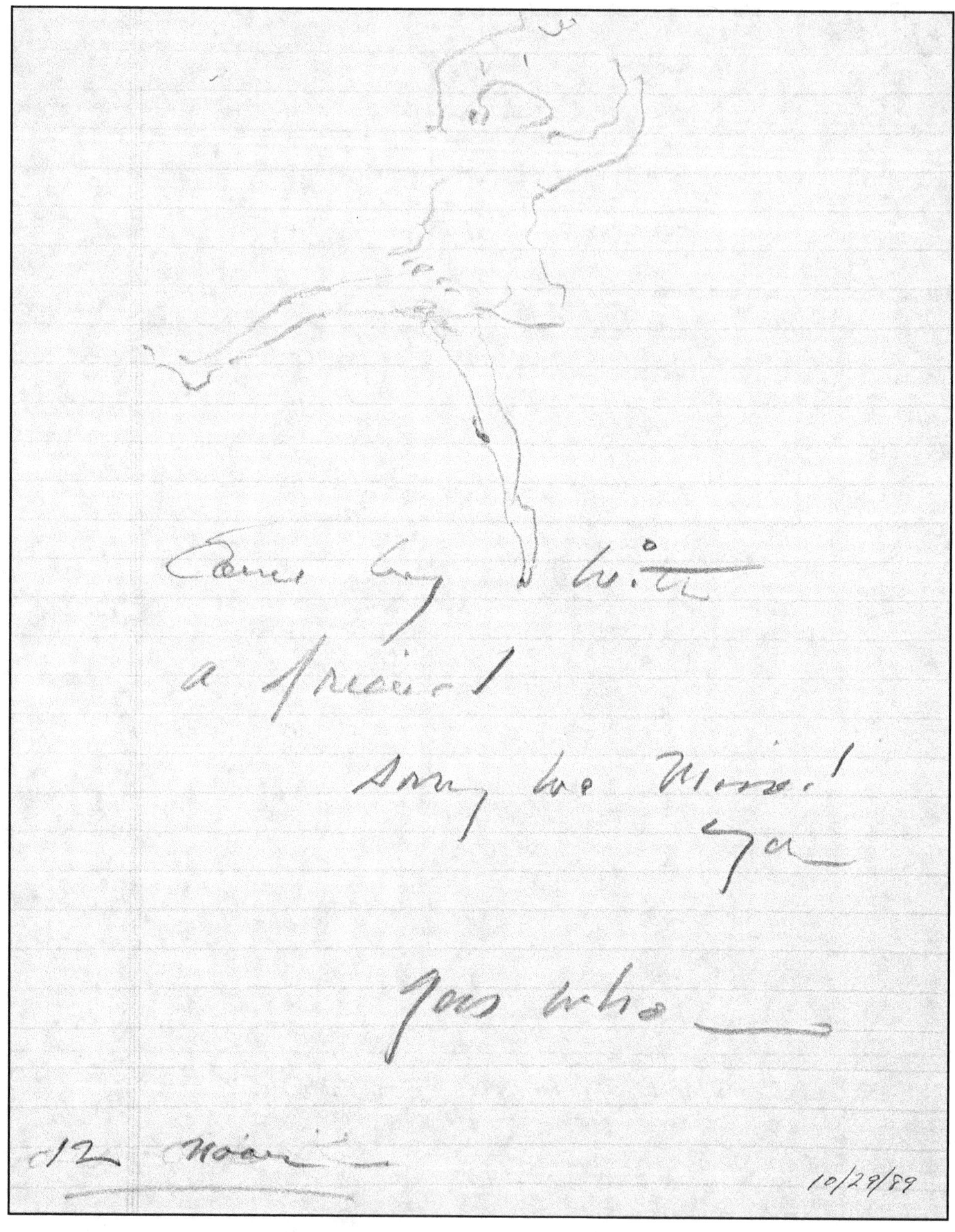

10/29/89   "Came by with a friend" from "Guess who?"

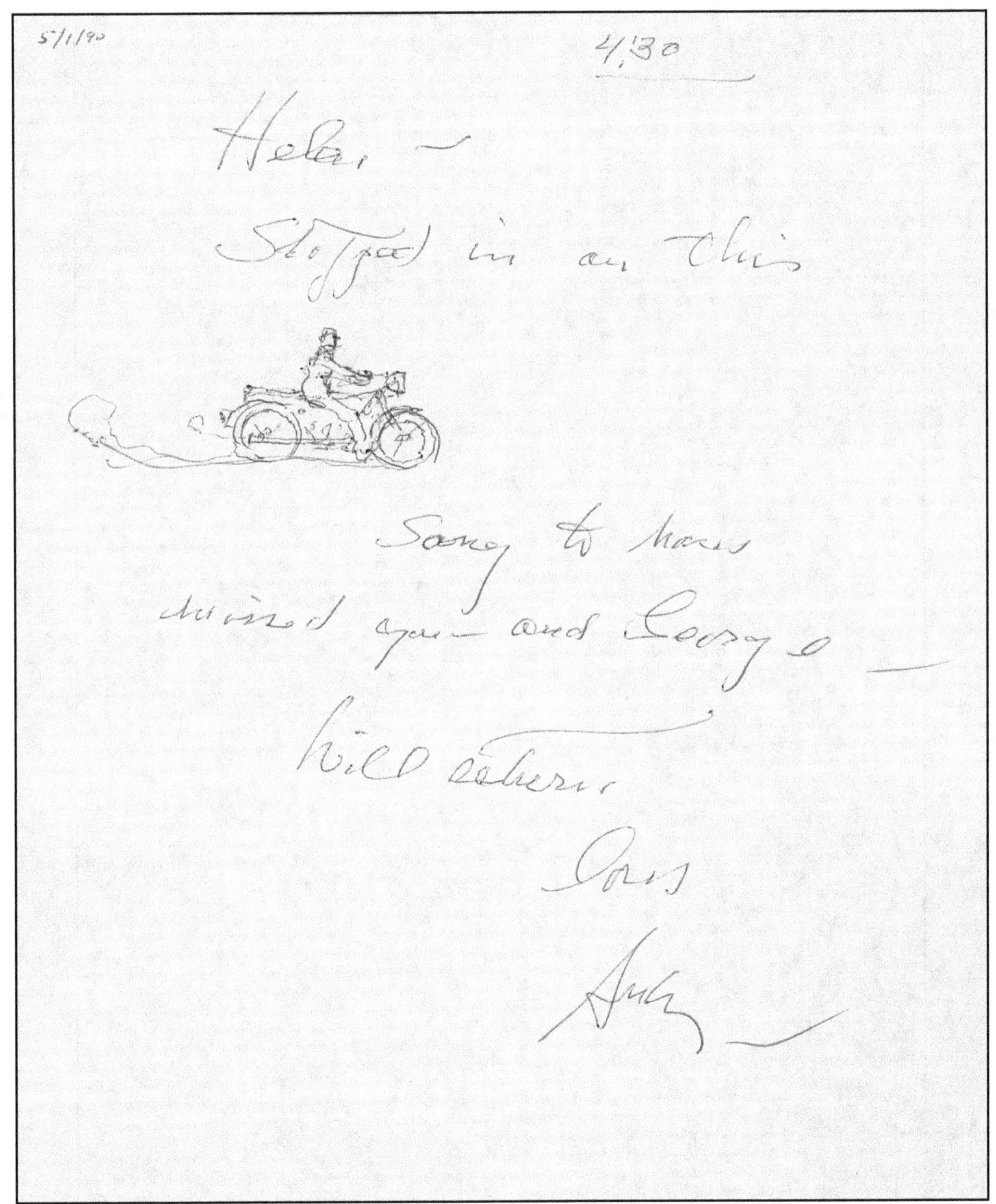

5/1/90   *Stopped by on motorcycle*

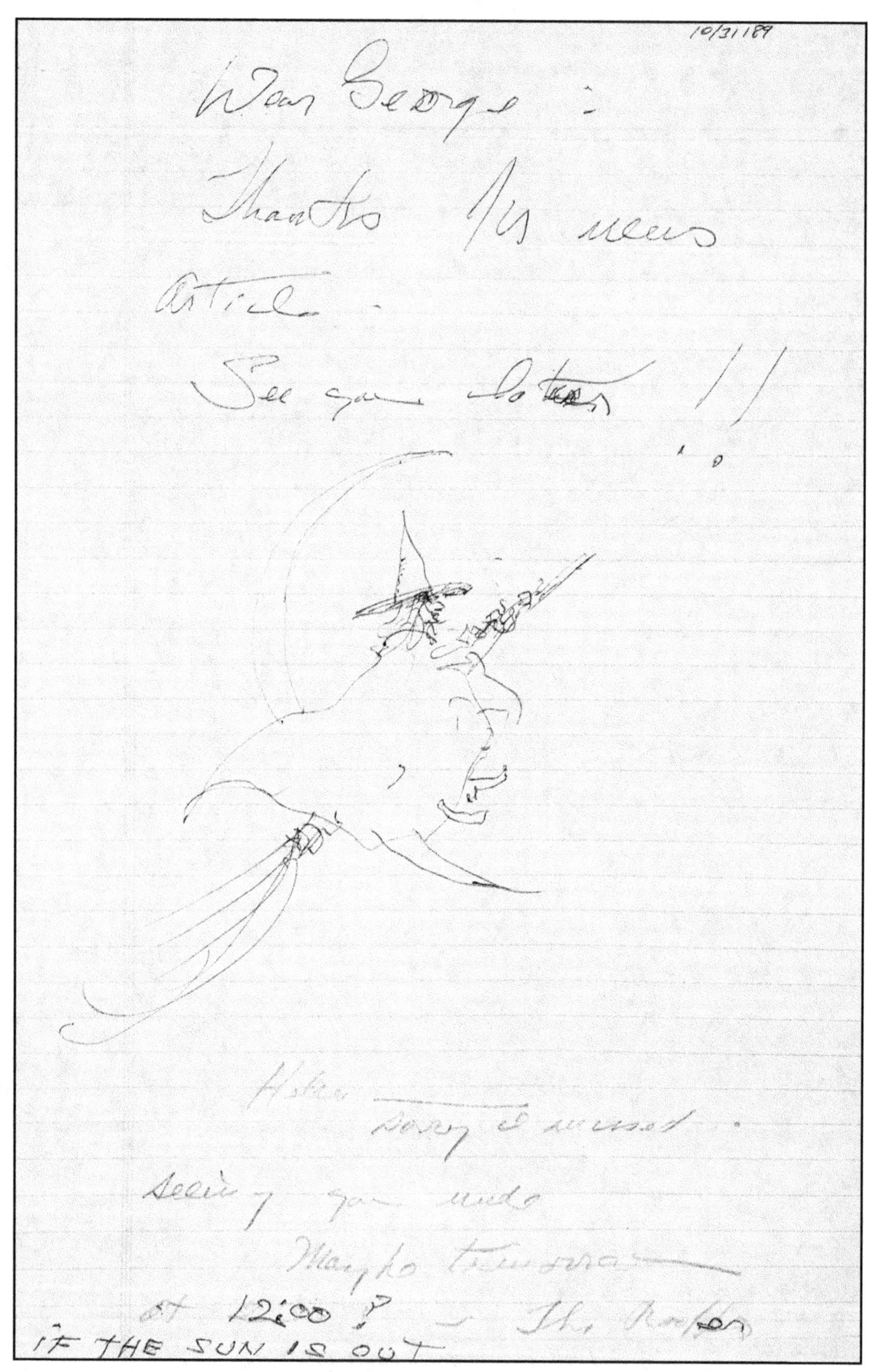

10/31/89   "Sorry I missed you." — "The Roofer"

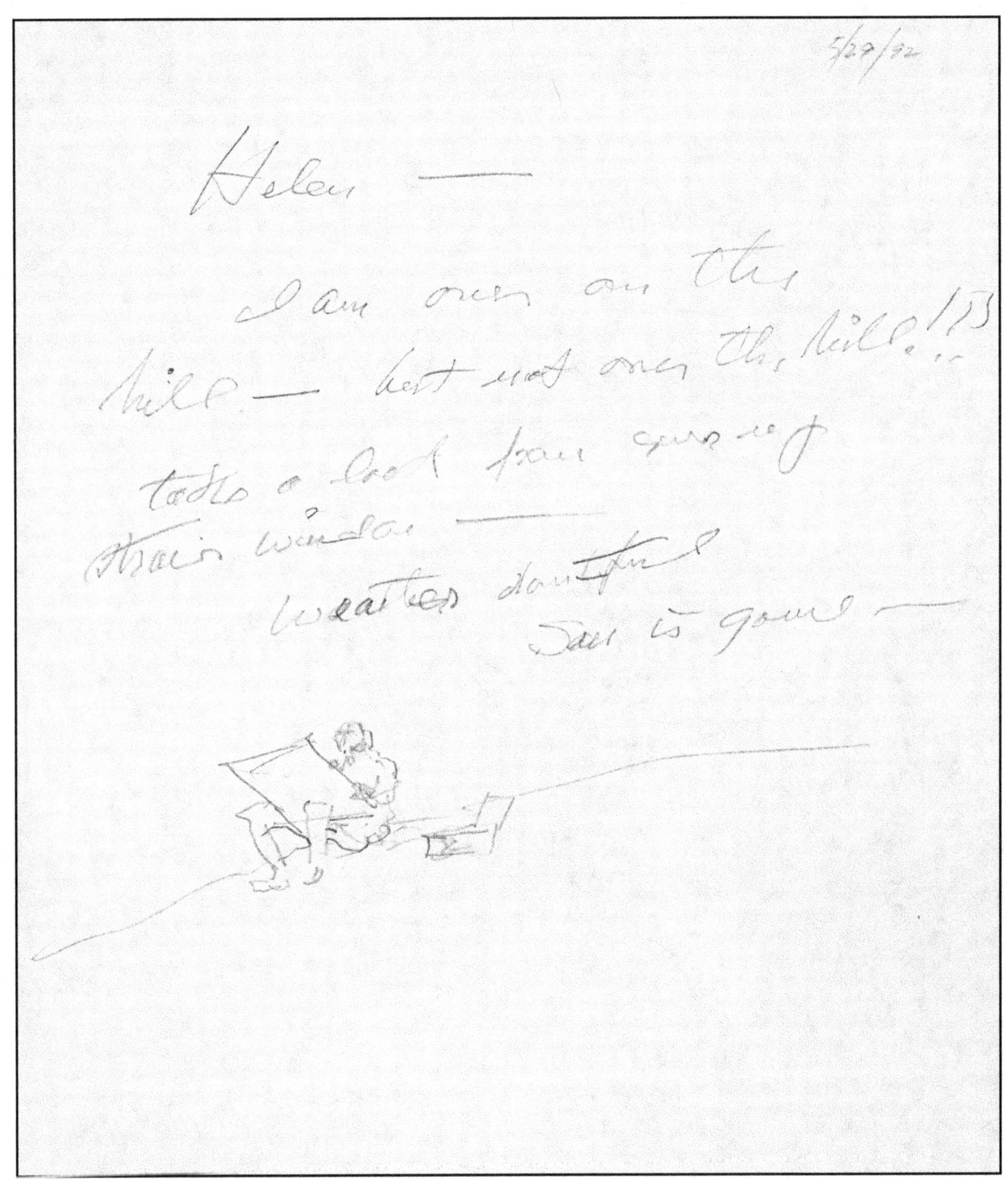

5/29/9   **"I'm over on the hill but not over the hill!!**

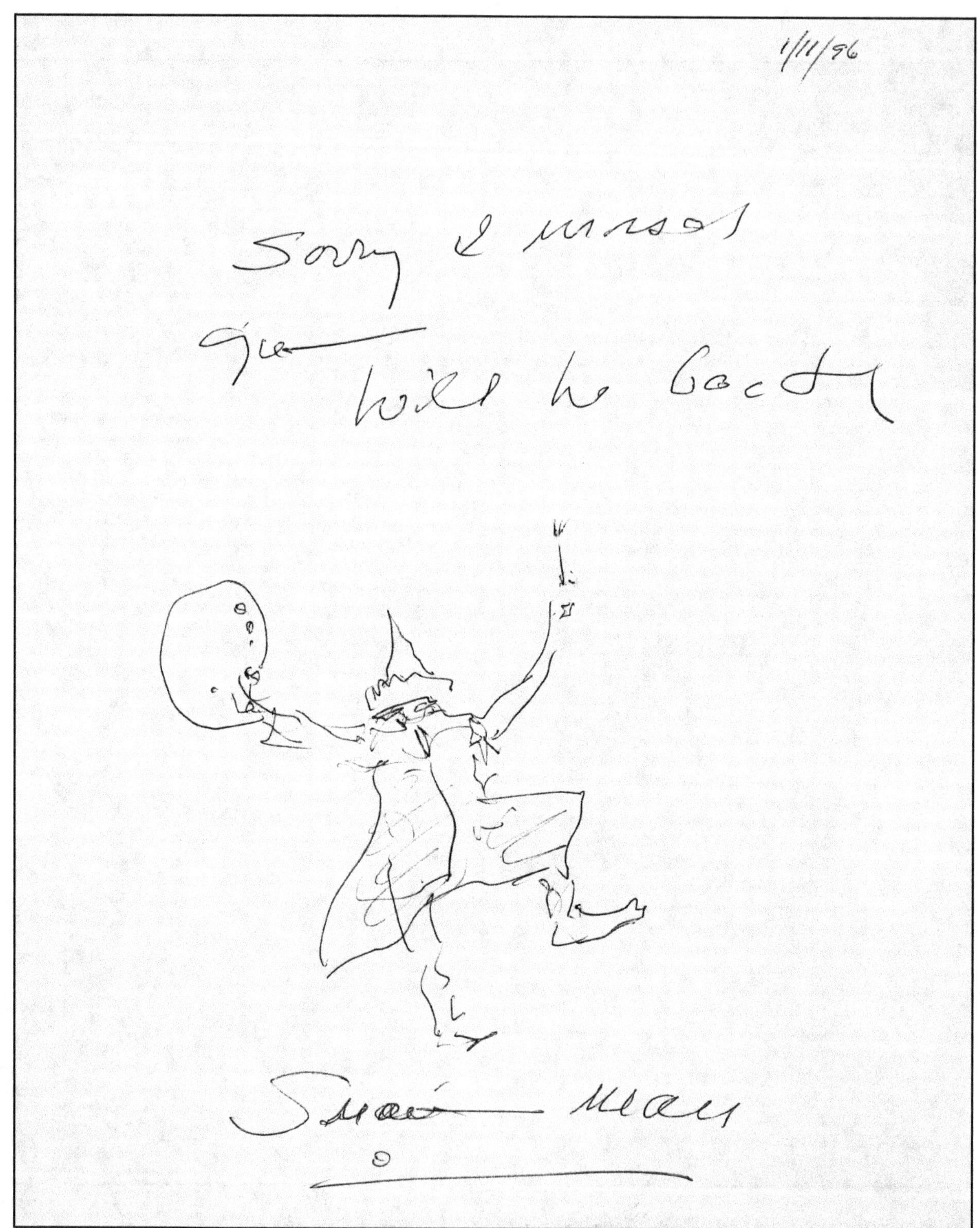

1/11/96   "Sorry I missed you"... "Snow Man"

Phyllis Diller

January 5, 1998

Dear Helen

There are no words to tell you the thrill your fabulous
dinner was for Stephanie and me.

It was so wonderful to meet such brilliant people, such
a civilized group.

Stephanie is so inspired by the meeting she is making an
in-depth study of Andrew Wyeth and his methods and history.

I am totally enchanted with Andrew and Betsy and would
love to have their address so I can write to them and
tell them how much I enjoyed being with them.

You and your husband have created the most gorgeous
warm haven in that beautiful home.

It was such a pleasure to see your Christmas decorations
and the way you have brought that grand old house into
the 20th century in such a creative way.

Your dinner was one of the high points of our lives.

Thank you. Have a great New Year.

Love

Phyllis

P.S.   Please give names to your dinner guests on
the enclosed snap shots.

*PS — When you travel out this way
please let me know. I'd like
to entertain you.
PD*

1/5/98   A "Thank you" letter.

My dear Helen & George —
Needless to say I miss
you both.
It's been a very cold winter
here but very beautiful
and exciting to me.
A week ago I drove in
to your drive, or should say
sled in and out on ice
at Painters Folley —

I am sending you a watercolor —
my love to Susie and Marty
and to you
all
Andy —

Feb 13, 2003

Here I am
trying to make a drawing
on Sugar Soap — as George would
say freezing my ass off

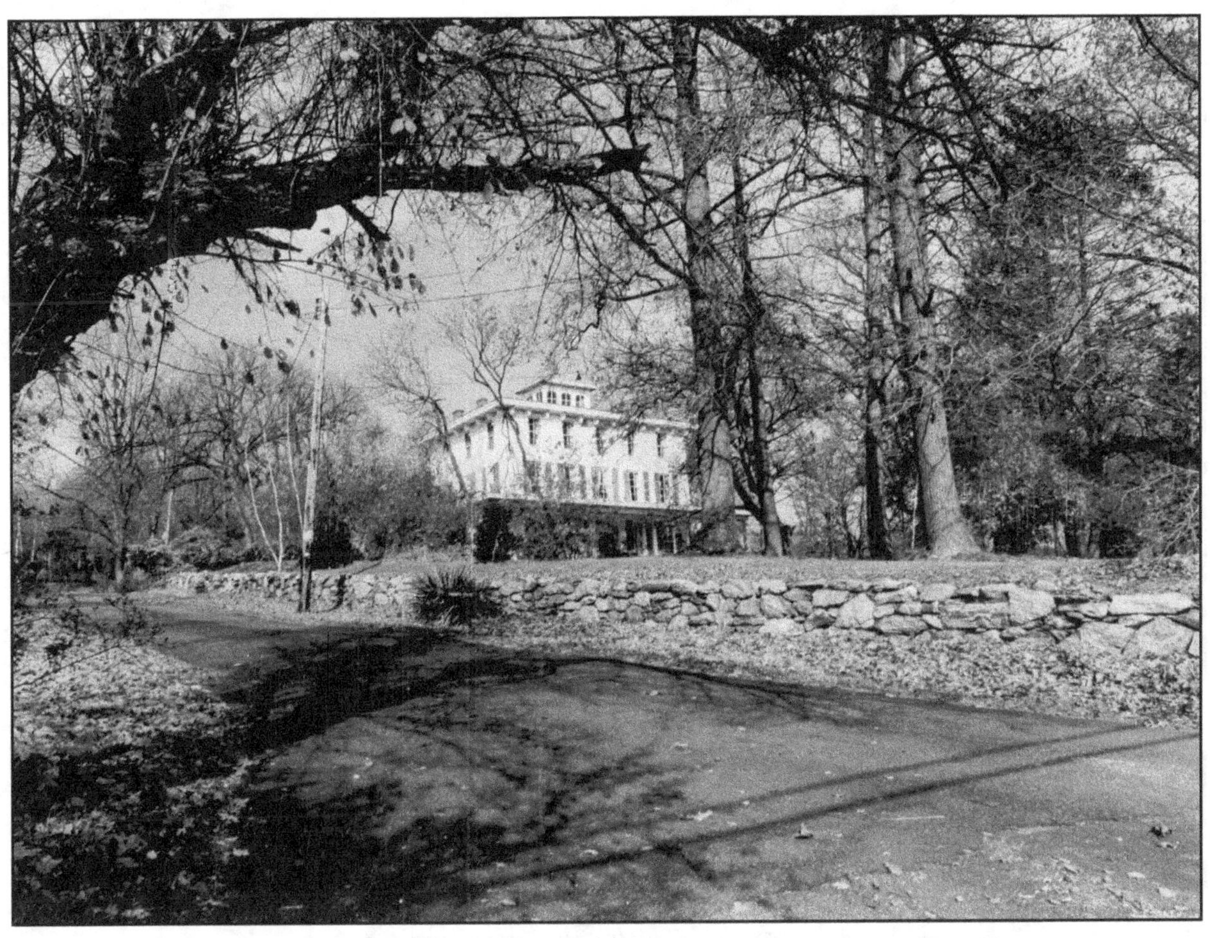

Painter's Folly

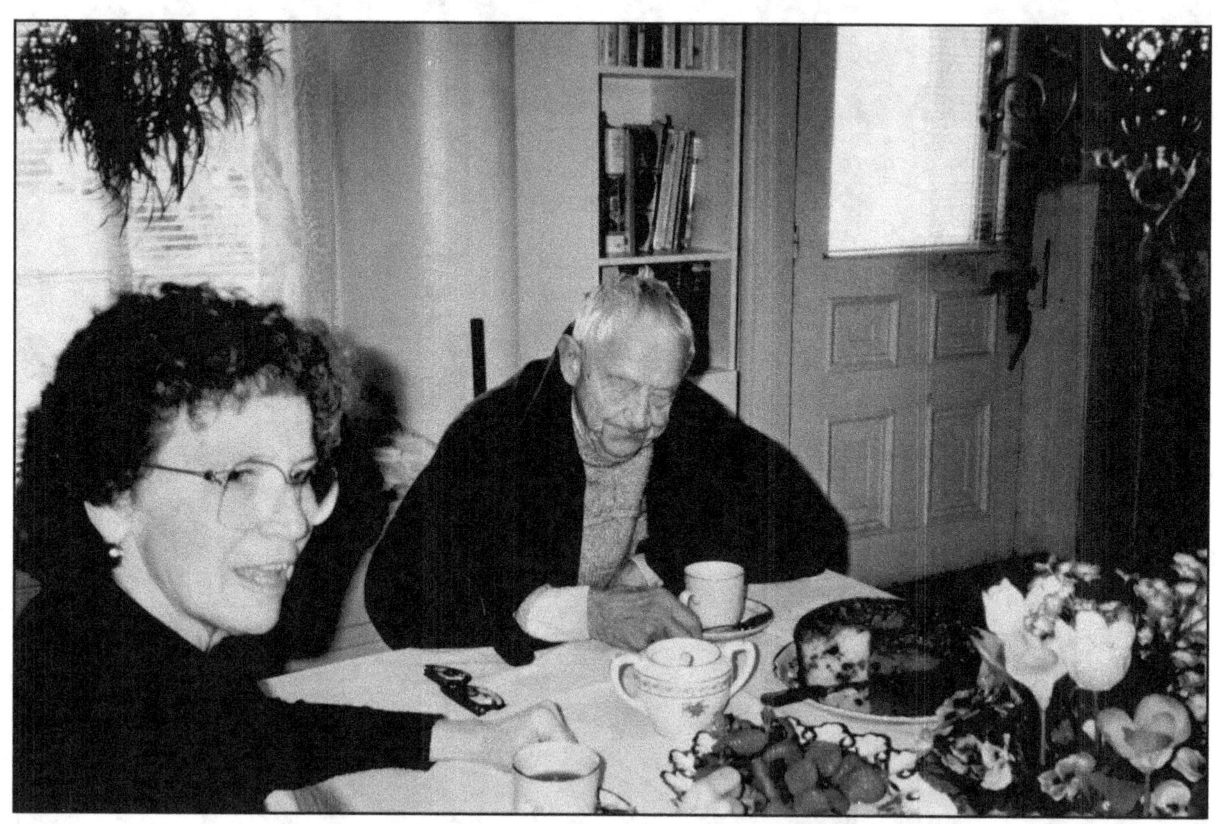

Helen & Andy with usual morning tea.

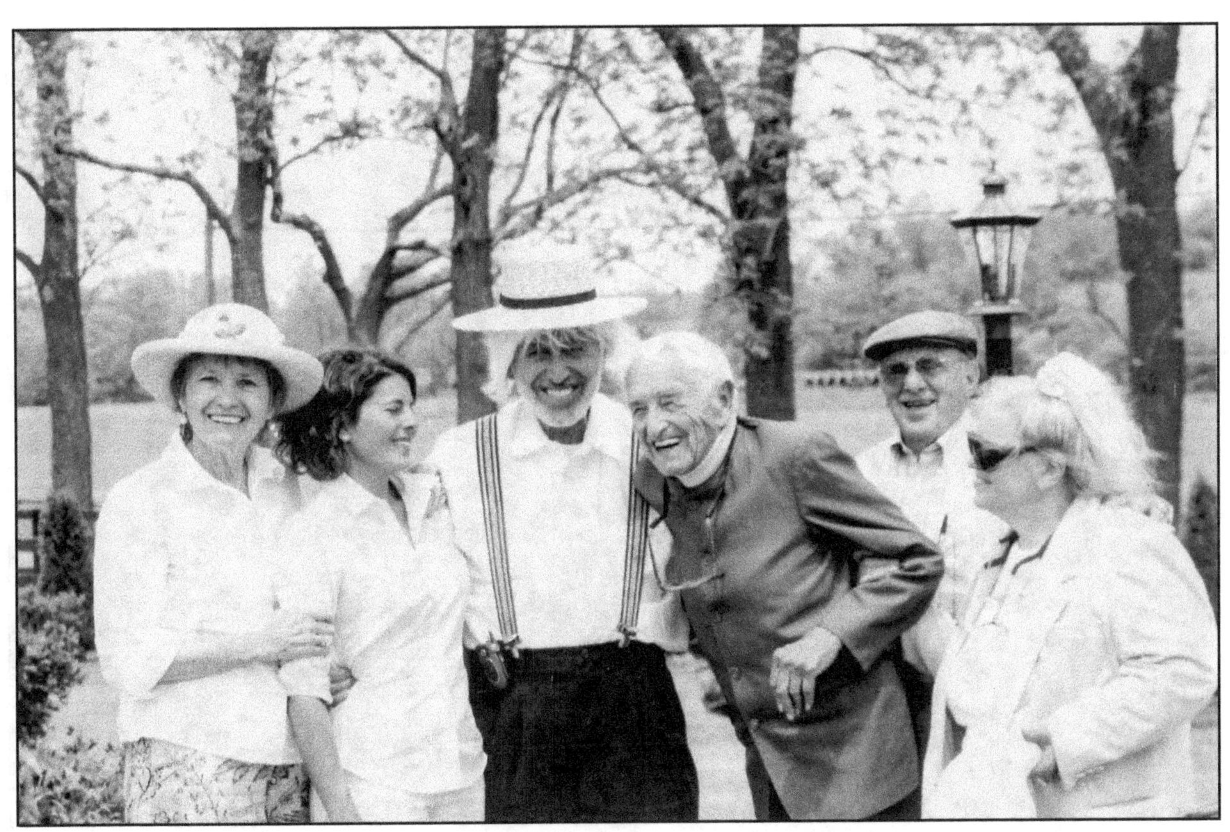

2008   Helen, Lisa & Peter Coggins, Andy, George & Helga playing joke on Andy.

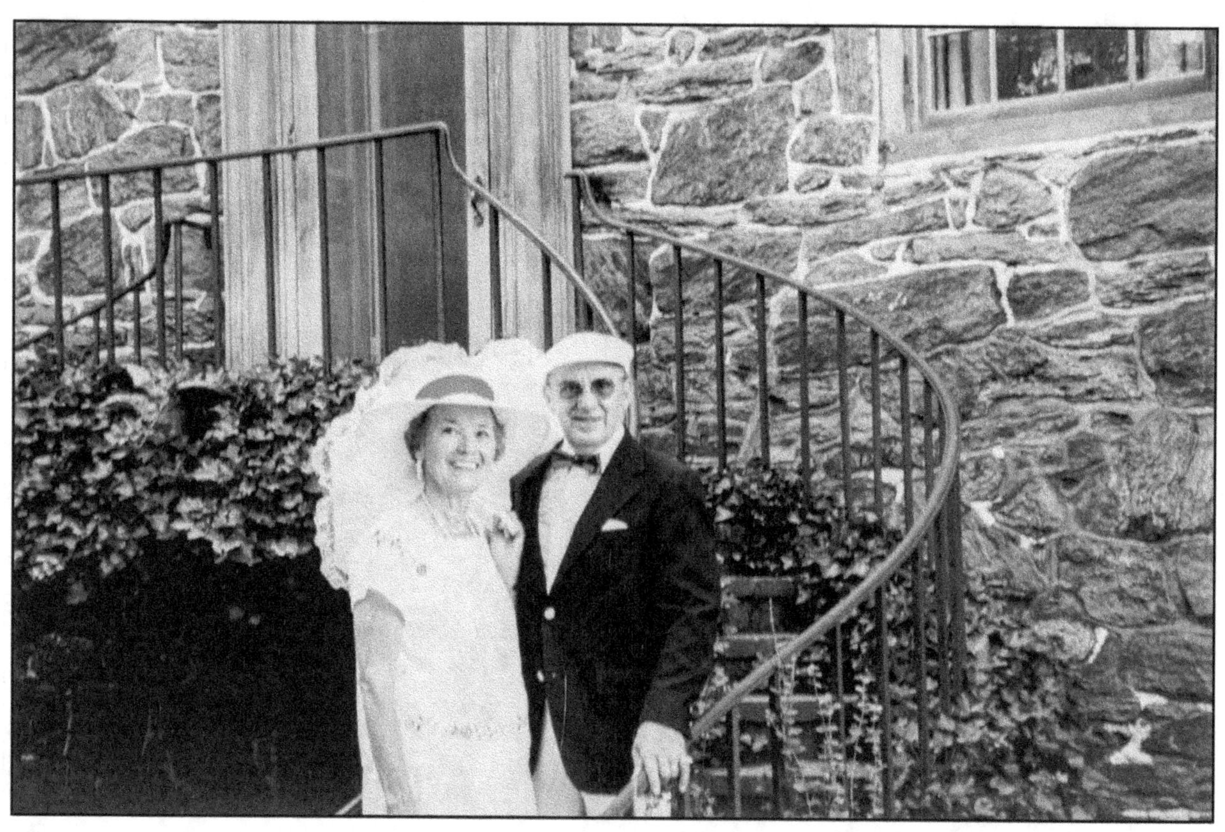

2001 - Helen & George Sipala at Frolic Weymouth's Garden party.

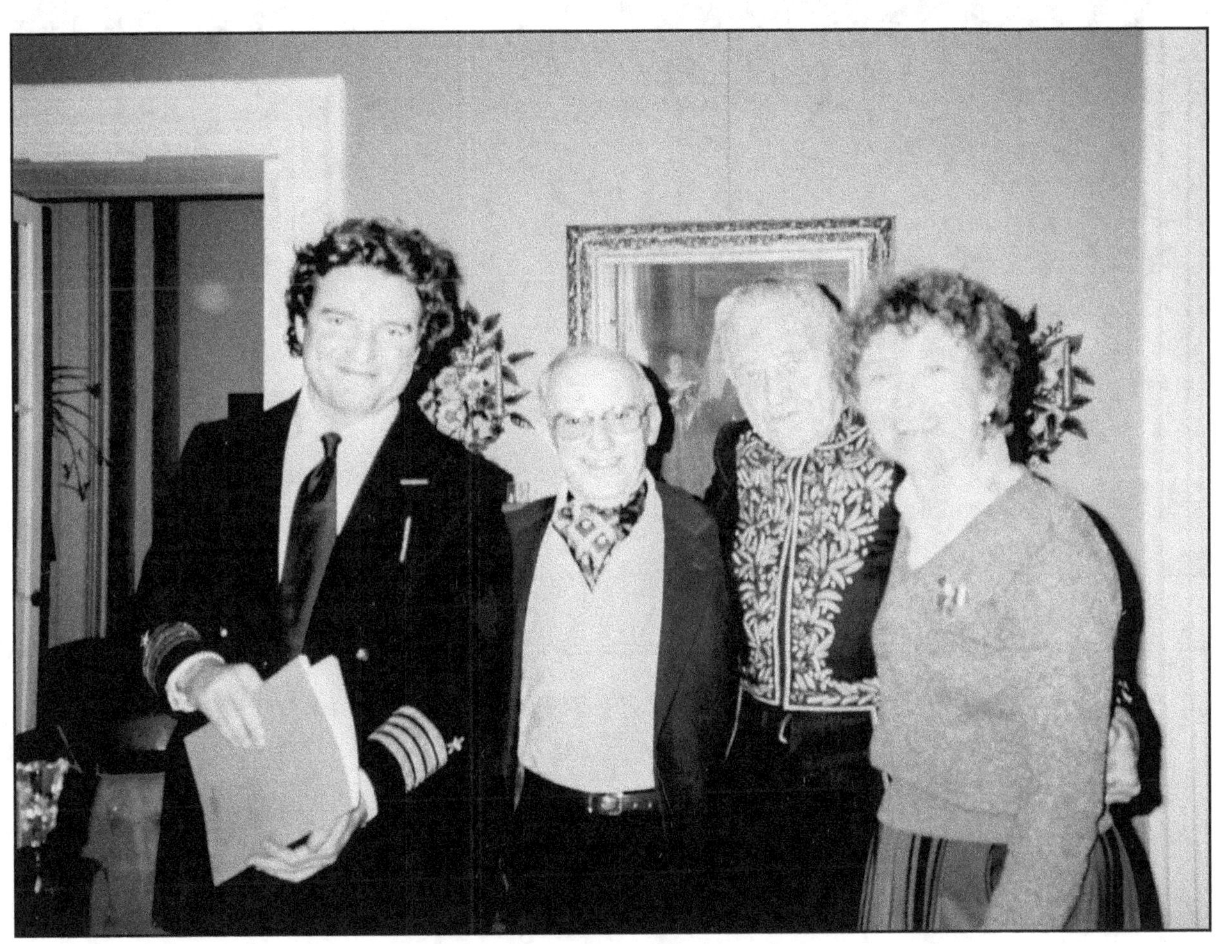

*12/10/89   Jamie Wyeth, George, Andy & Helen at 1st dinner party at the Sipala's.
Note formal attire Andy wore to impress us!*

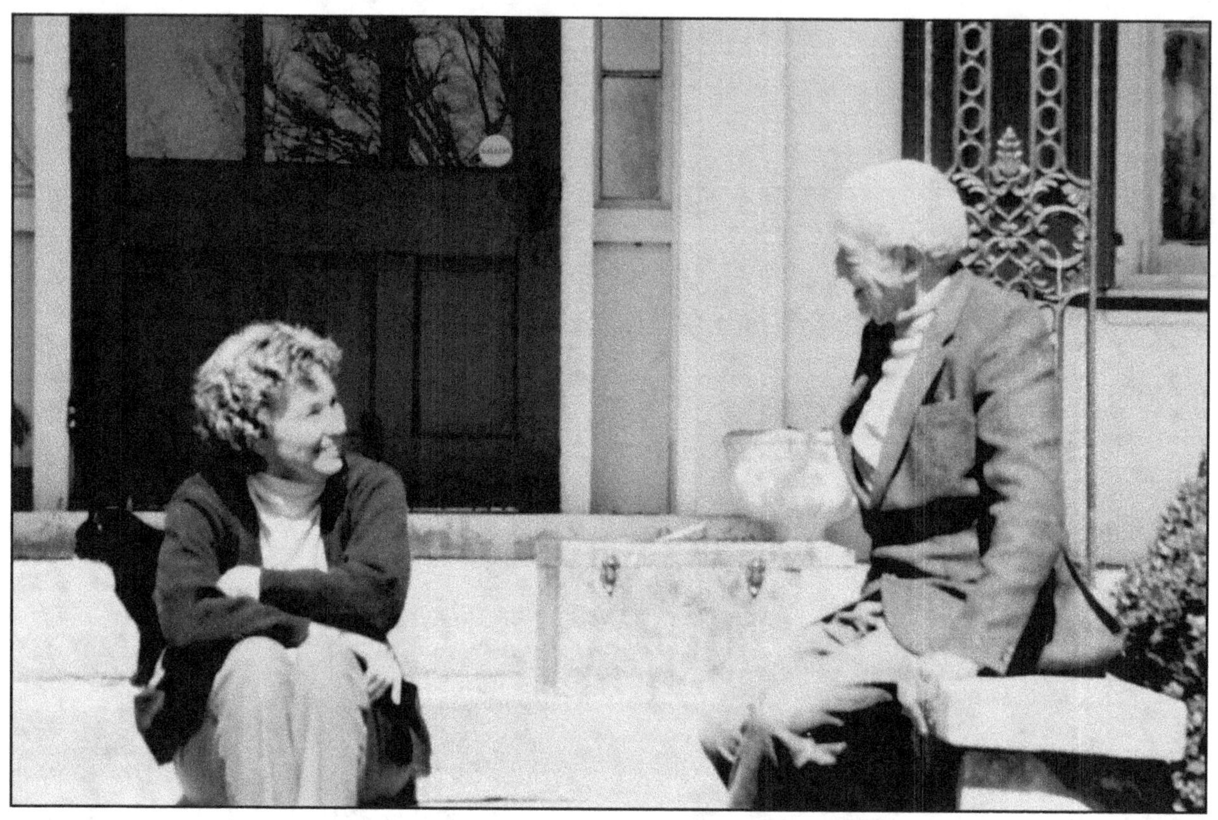

*3/1990   Helen & Andy enjoying the sun on Painter's Folly's front porch.
Note the paint box.*

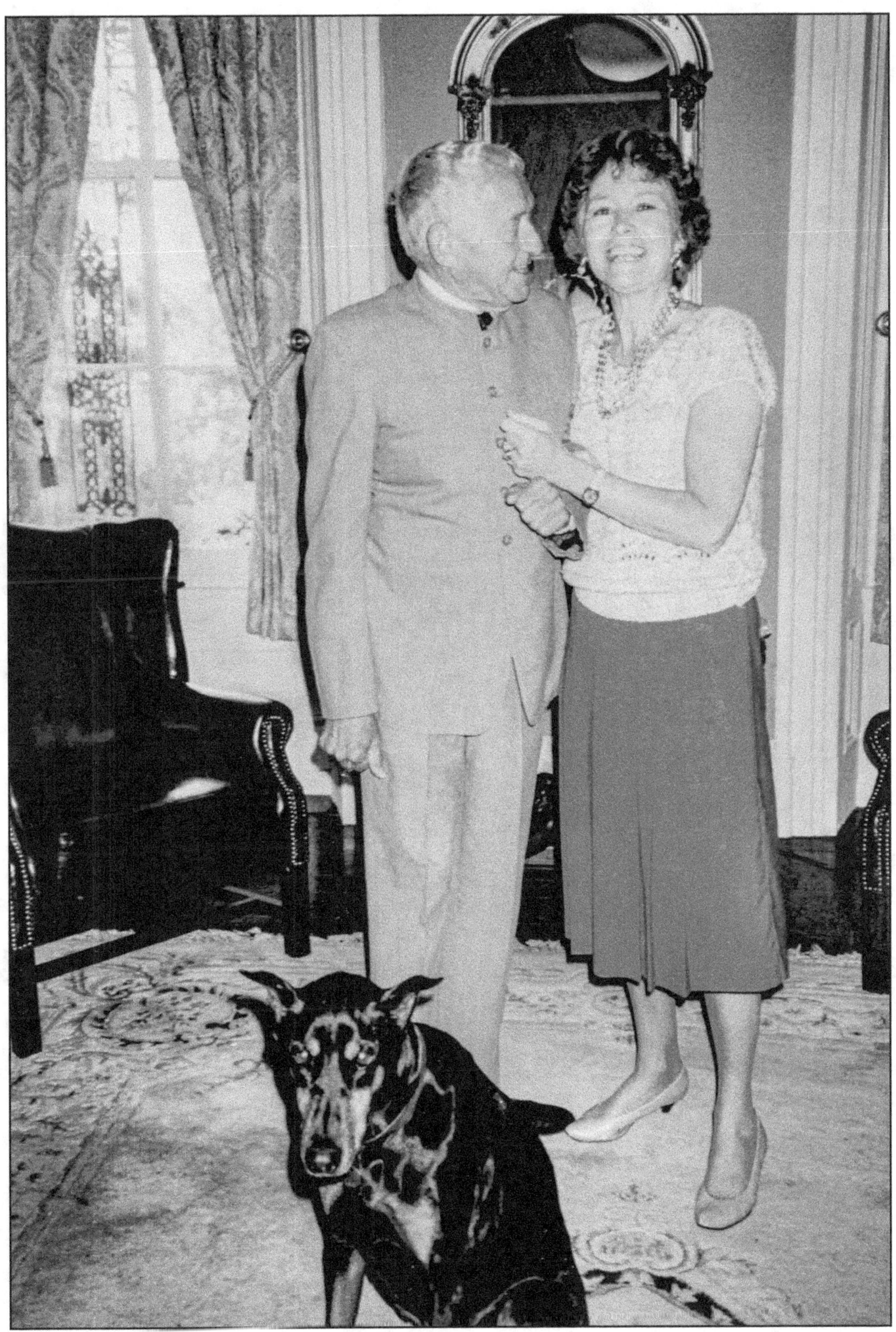

5/31/90Andy is proud to show us his favorite Nehru style suit on his way to N.Y. for an award at the Russian Embassy.

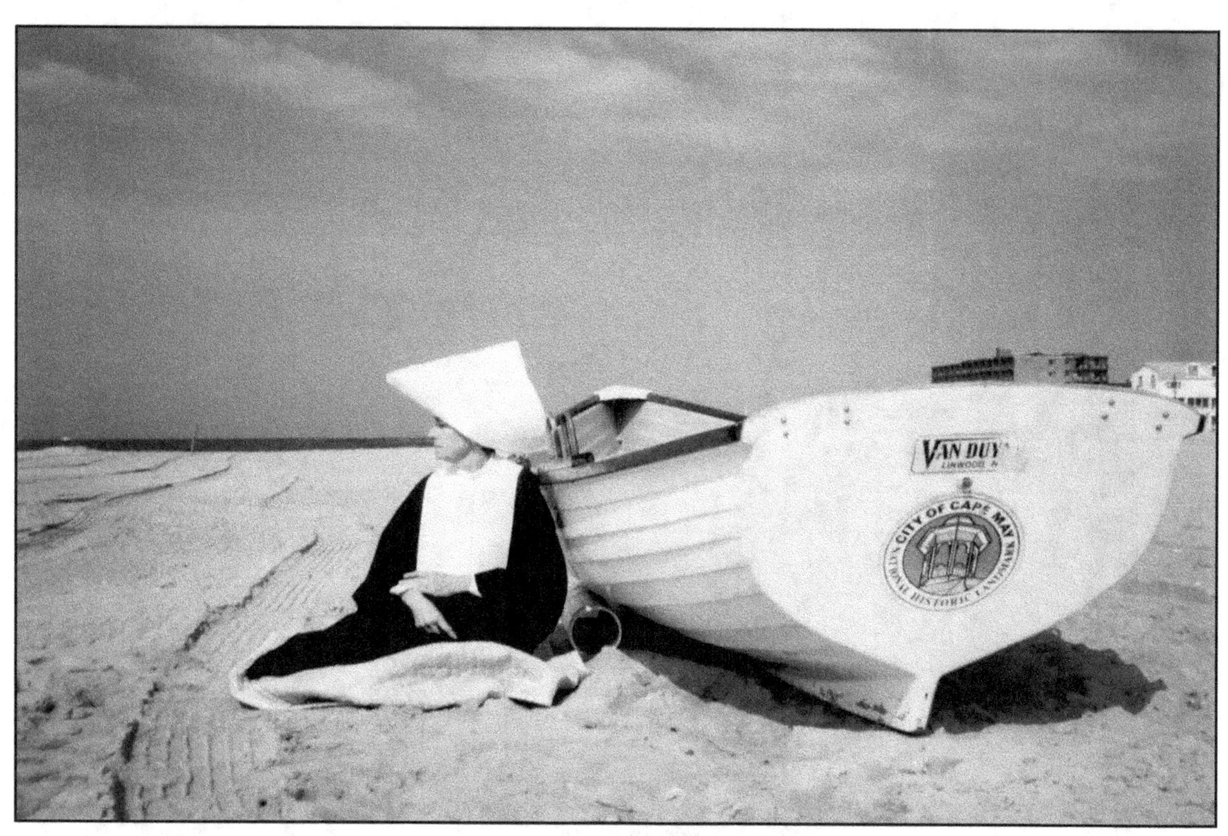

6/16/92   Helen posing for "Cape May" painting.

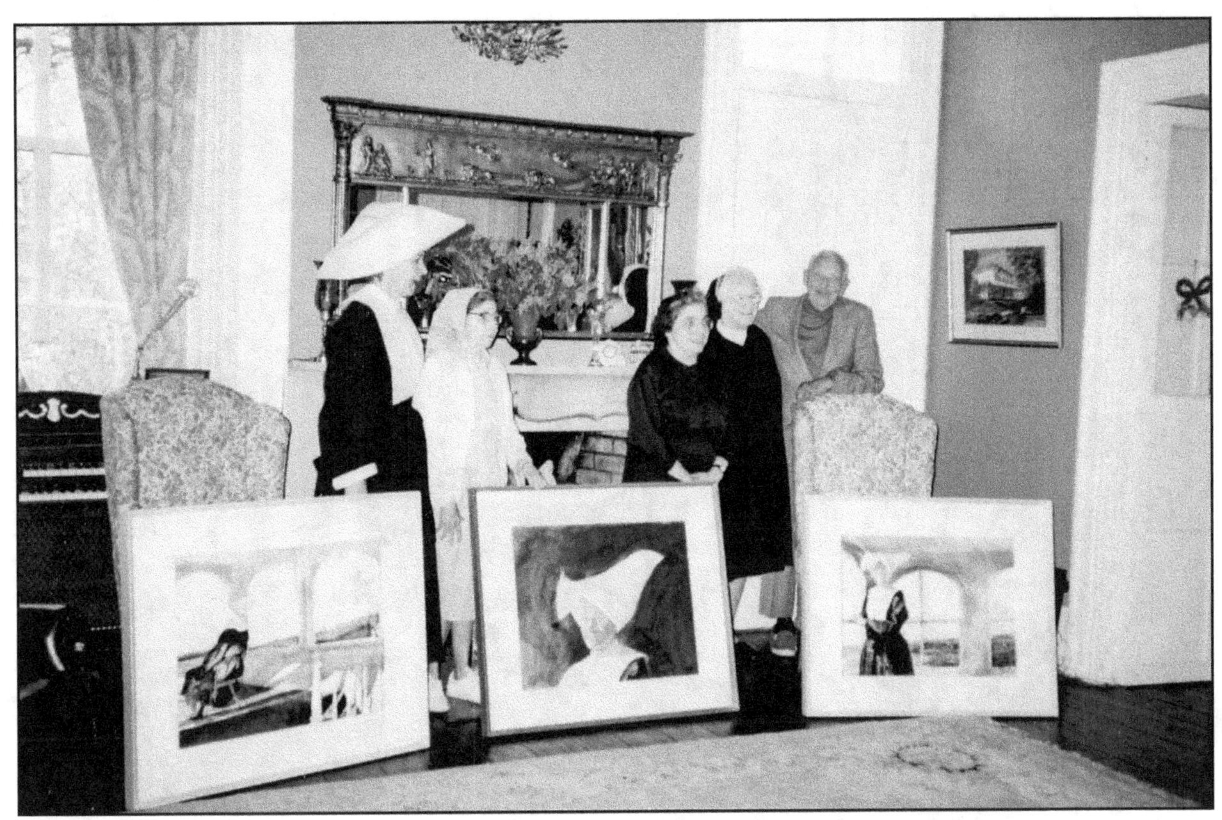

5/7/92   Helen (in habit) with Sisters of Charity and Andy admiring series of his nun paintings.

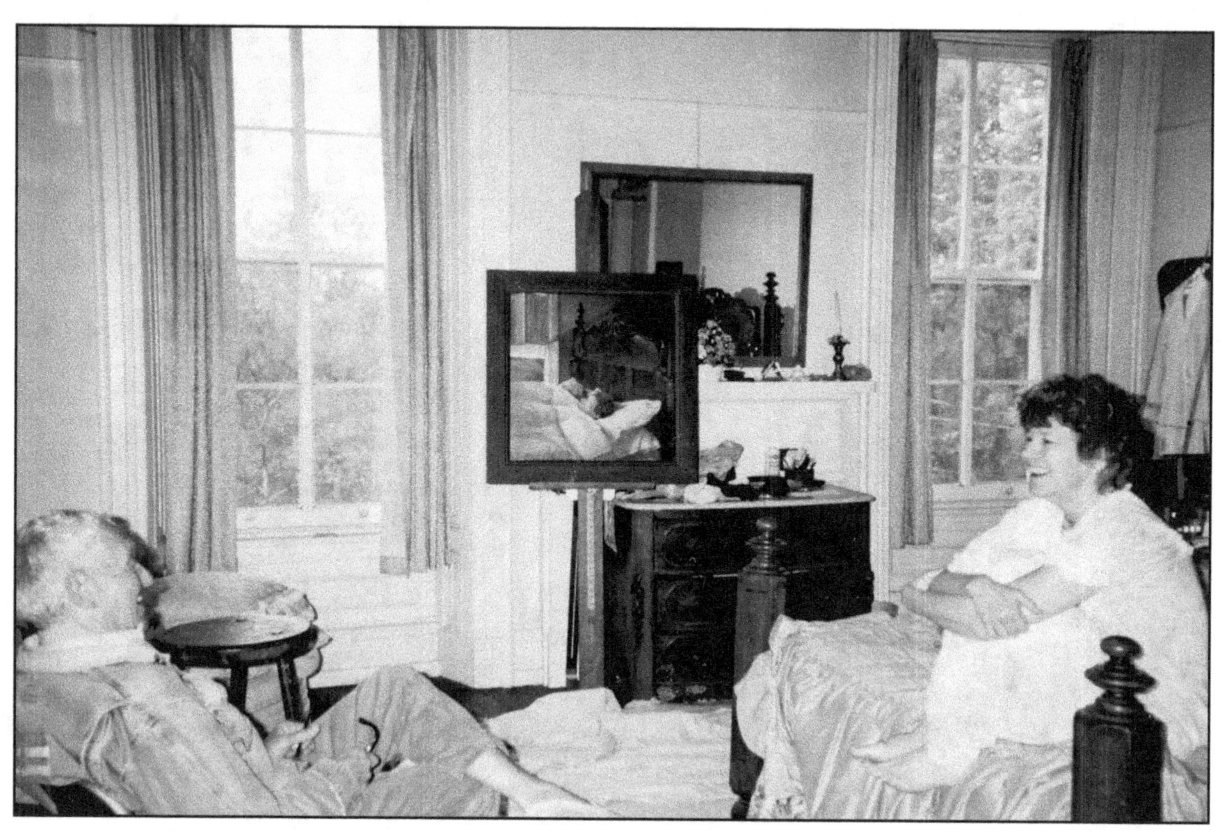

3/4/93   Andy and Helen admiring finished painting of MARRIAGE.

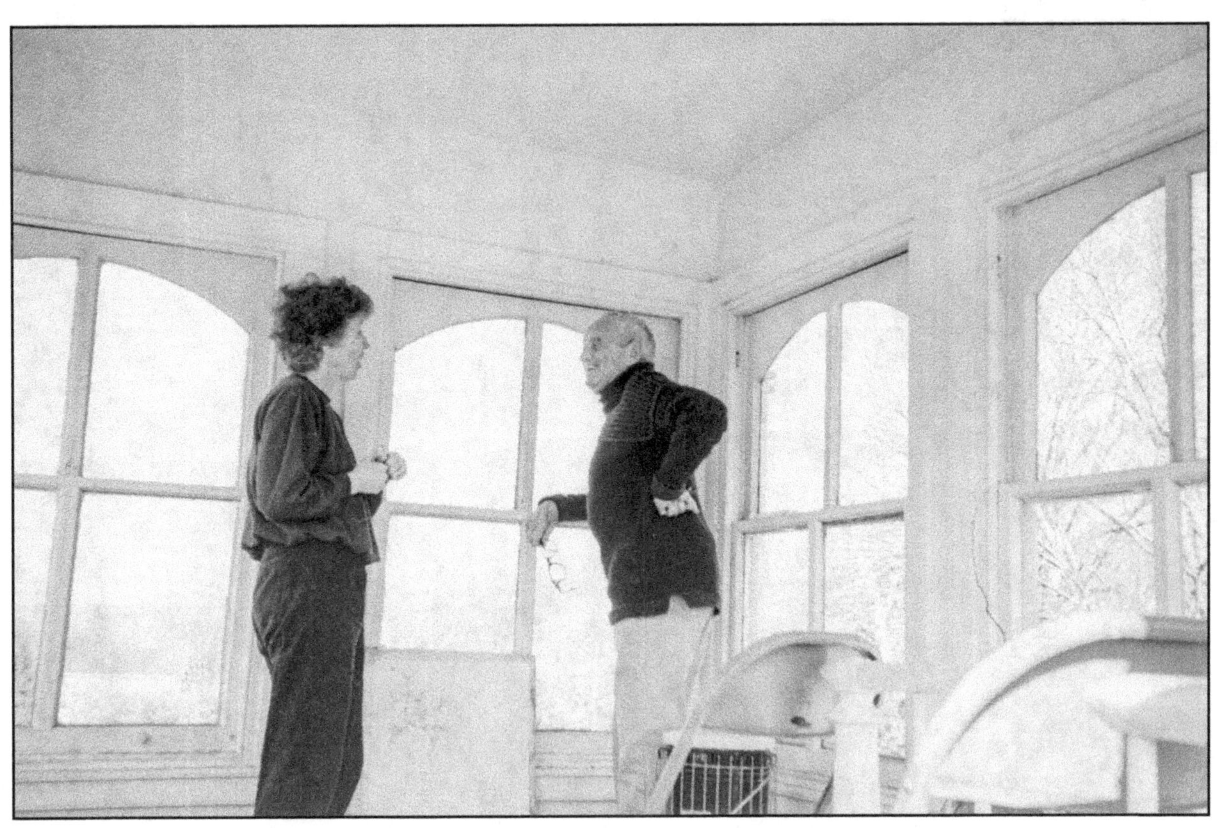

1995   Helen and Andy enjoying the Widow's Walk.

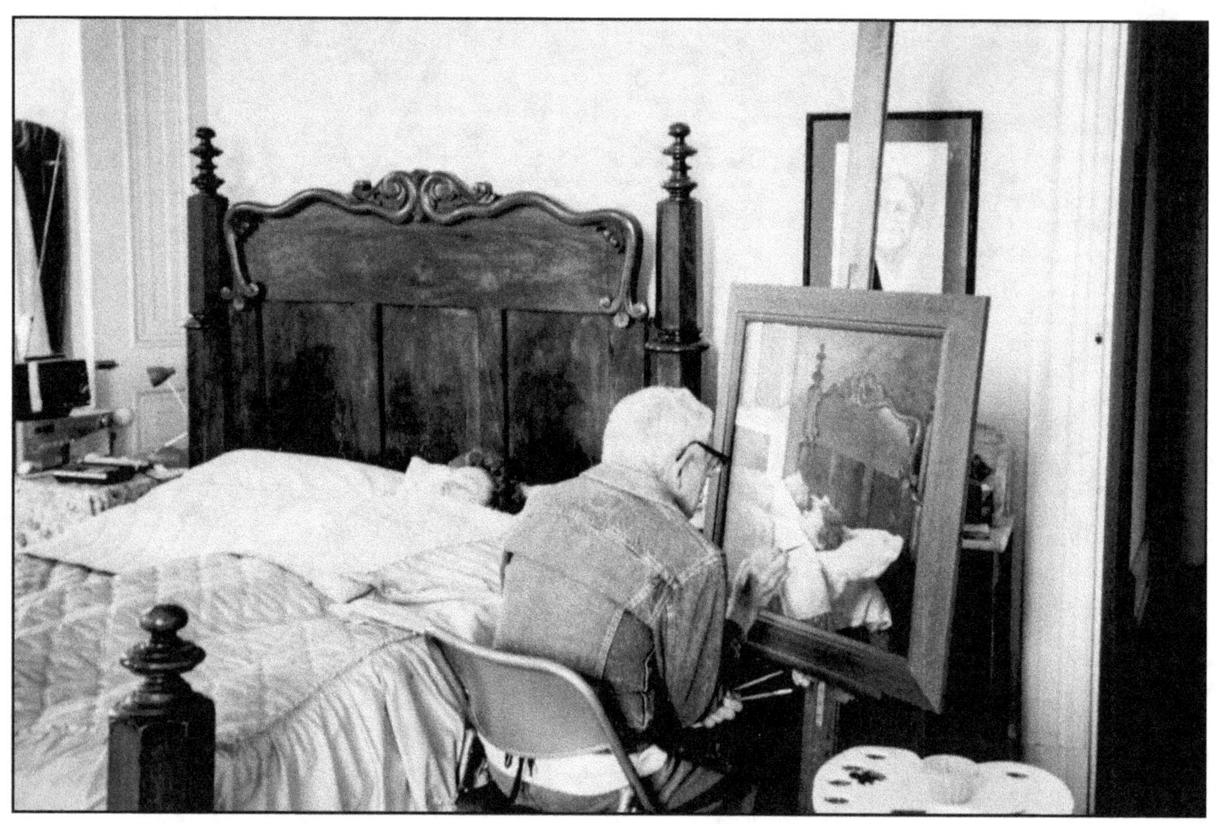

March 1993   Helen's turn to pose for MARRIAGE.

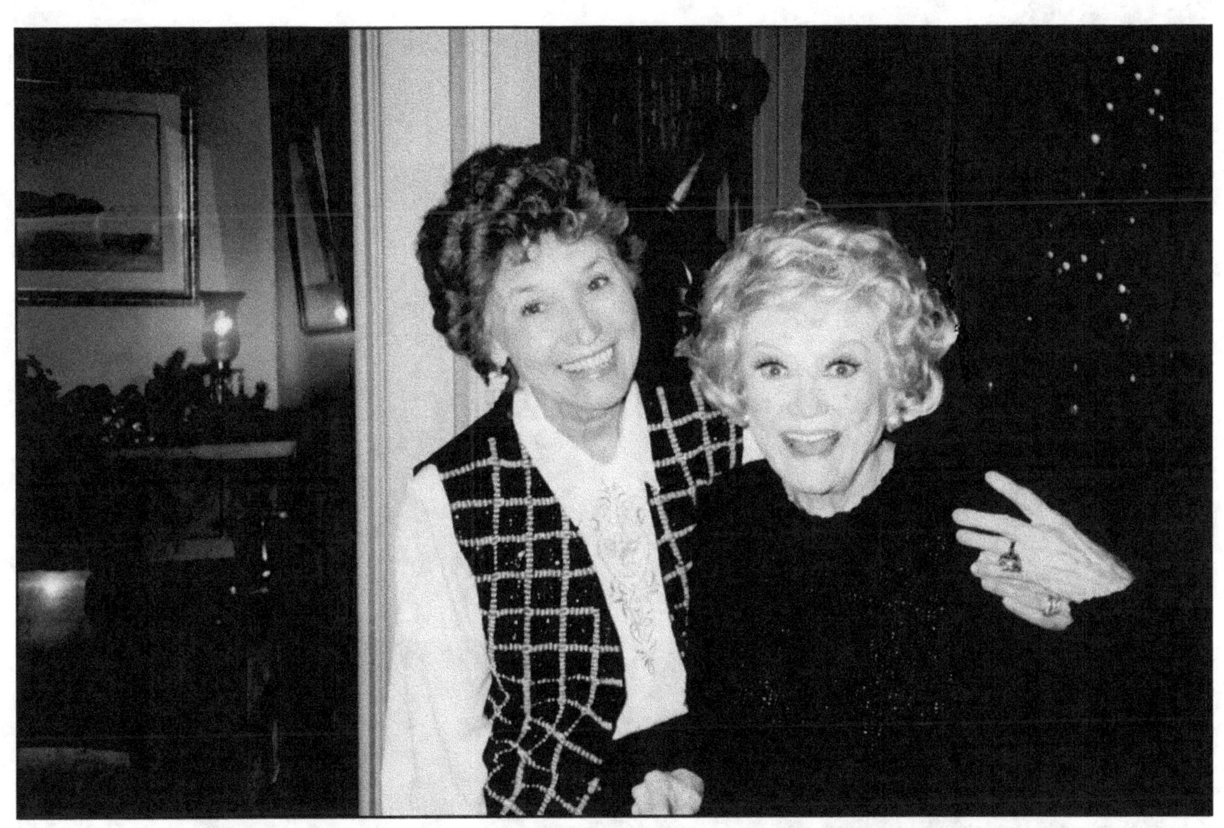

Dec. 1999   Helen & Phyllis Diller at Helen's dinner party.

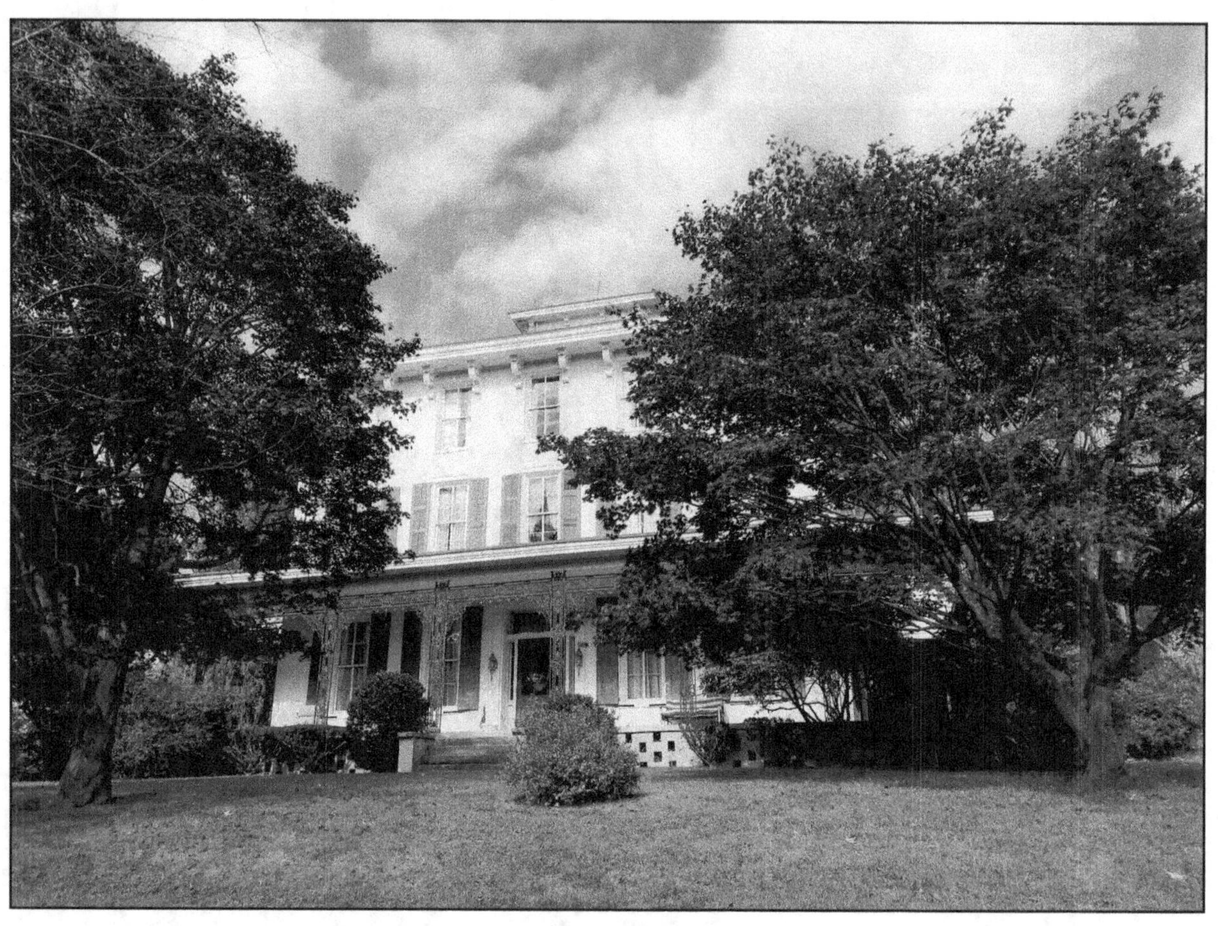

Painter's Folly

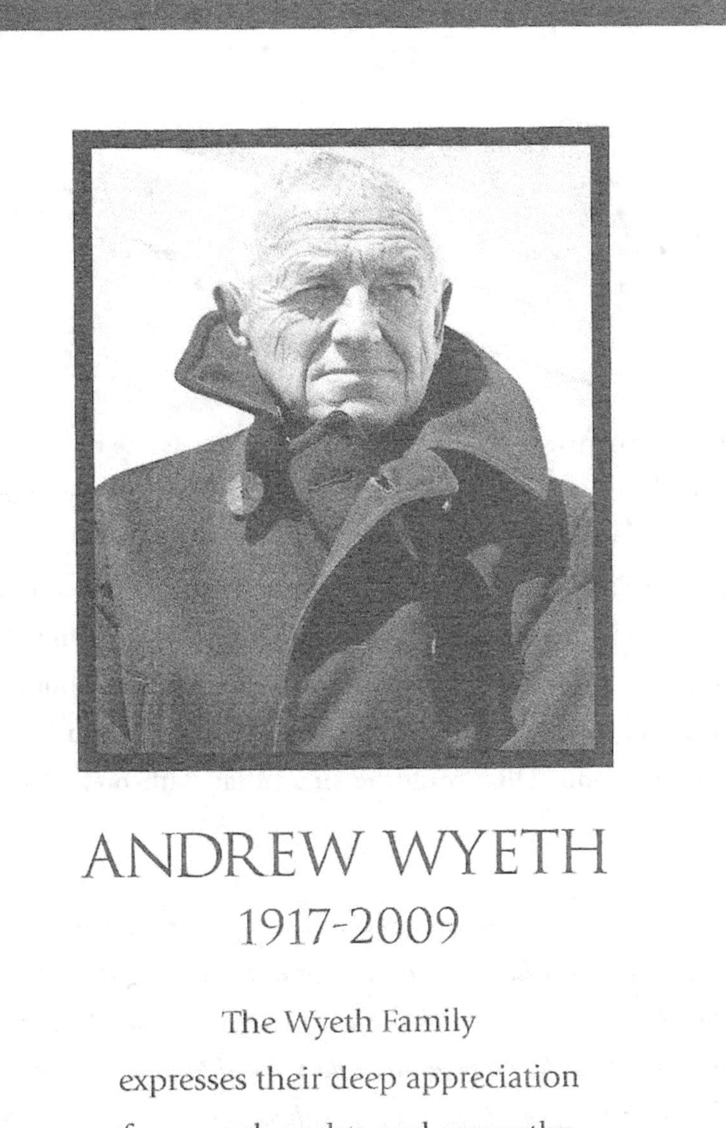

ANDREW WYETH
1917-2009

The Wyeth Family

expresses their deep appreciation

for your thoughts and sympathy.

CHAPTER SIX
1994

Life's Fragilities

Helen's distrust of Andy's stories continued as the new year began. "He says what he thinks you want to hear," Helen wrote. She even doubted Andy's plea that he was suffering from the flu.

Helen especially wished Andy would stop telling her tales about women. "I detest the stories he tells me about women," Helen wrote. One of those stories was about a former model who supposedly seduced Andy about 40 years ago. Helen wrote, "He thought it funny and I laughed with him but was appalled with this information! How could he share that with me? Shame, shame on him!"

January 5: Andy was disappointed that I was home yesterday because of snow and he didn't know it. He told me to ring three times when I'm home and he'll come up. I won't do that. Besides, it gives me a real free day alone. I don't need to give him therapy time. Painting, yes. Psychiatrist's couch, no.

January 9: Andy called and has no electricity. There was an ice storm. He and Betsy stay by the fireplace and cook on the grille.

January 12: Our Xmas gift dinner for the Wyeths: Jim Barnes, owner of the Dilworthtown Inn personally, with his wine steward, delivered our pre-arranged dinner. Jim had the menu done in calligraphy and added chocolate truffles. Wyeths were excited and impressed by it all.

January 22: He is proud of Nicky. Nicky is like Andy and Jamie like

*Betsy. Today he gets on the subject of his being a spirit. "I am
nothing, no body, absolutely worthless, he insists. "I agree, that
is how I will remember you." When I mention that perhaps
he is referring to a "here after" he objects adamantly. He can't
stand religion, churches or preachers. "They are so banal." I
pray silently that Jesus will give me words for him. We hit on
the subject of the value of education. He says it is worthless
and we've all ruined ourselves with it. I disagree. For the first
time today he said he's ashamed of himself for his past and his
weaknesses. He's not proud of himself for a lot he has done other
than painting. I was amazed and told him so. I think the ice
has broken and God is beginning to shine on him and he isn't
aware. Thank God, for now."*

*February 5: He shows up, eager to show us his new painting of hands
in ice. We love it completely! His idea is taken in part from the
N. C. Wyeth book of old Lynch's drowning near the mill. Andy
is excited about the large chunks of ice in the race that the flood
deposited. He places the bronze hands of himself on the ice and
paints.*

Valentine's Day brings an exchange of gifts between the Wyeths and the
Sipalas. Candy, Valentine cards, chocolate waffles and a pair of crazy glasses
with paper eyes changed hands. Andy also gave Helen Channel #5 perfume.
"You'll see me when you see me," Andy said upon parting.

*Note: I hate writing this diary! It's too time consuming and I get
behind in it. I forget some interesting facts. Will anyone be
interested in such trivia?*

One day with snow swirling, Andy busily sketched the roof, chimney and
Lafayette's Headquarters from widow's walk.

*February 26: I'm getting tired of his persistence, digs and dread
his visits. I cannot really speak my mind as it might ruin our
relationship and Wyeth connections. It was Alys Cort's birthday
party at Frolic's barn. Present were the Rockefellers, du Ponts,*

Hewitts, Wyeths and lots of "beautiful people." We sent flowers with balloons. A real privilege to be there!

February 27: He brought a tempera painting of a sleigh in a barn. It was gorgeous. A very first showing again. He doesn't stay long. Carolyn had another stroke.

March 2: He brings news that Carolyn died at 3 am yesterday. The nurses were combing her hair and fussing over her as she was near death. She turned her head from left to right, facing them and half spit/half blew at them as a grand finale and passed away. A very befitting end to such a tough woman. Helga helped prepare her.

March 6: He is not happy with the subject matter without the storm affect. He erases everything and gives up. "Just a pretty picture; might as well have Santa Claus on the chimney."

March 9: Light snow. He is jockeying for a private room at the National Gallery for his paintings. "I don't want them in the basement gathering dust." Several museums are contacting him. He's thrilled and excited.

March 11: He has been to Media to clear out Carolyn's estate. Today he plays 'Andrew Wyeth' to the hilt! He is bubbly. He jokes. He orchestrates and directs the final say in Carolyn's estate with boldness and power and surprises even himself. "Close the account and make no money on it." He keeps Eight Bells and gives the rest to the Brandywine Museum. … I condemn him for tormenting me and he talks from the heart. He praises my lifestyle and speaks deeply of honoring me and placing me on a pedestal. He knows he is spoiled from wealth and fame and he is ashamed of his actions and free lifestyle.

The discussion turns to the Wyeth family of painters. Andy said, "I'm not as good a painter as my father but Jamie is not as good as me. I finish a painting and say the hell with it. Maybe it'll be good and maybe not." The conversation meandered from feelings to art to habits and emotions. Helen wrote that they love "those soul-searching moments. We treasure our friendship." The pair then talked about mortality.

*March 11: He feels all washed up and mentions quitting painting
again for the umpteenth time. Carolyn's death has brought him
back to reality and he is feeling life fading. He speaks of his own
death and laughingly suggests putting his ashes in a jar and
placing them on the mantel. A sober thought of life's fragilities.*

*March 19: Carolyn's death has affected him. Helga has a mental
crash and still wants to take food to Carolyn. She was really a
wild girl! She and Andy shared so many secrets and remained
very, very close forever. She was a real confidant.*

*April 12: He is in a rare mood today! He told us of the memorial
service for Carolyn. Each person scooped some of Carolyn's
ashes into the rocket until all was gone. Andy and Ann put
their fingers on the button and it blasted off. Jamie gave a
speech which was very touching, referring to the trees, birds and
favorites of Carolyn. The rocket carried out in the typical old
oriental custom. A white cloud of ashes floated over the front
yard. Andy kept the ornate box that contained the ashes. The
rocket blast was blamed for setting off Duff's house alarm down
the road.*

A family dispute was brewing in the Wyeth family. Betsy wanted to add a
dock to Eight Bells, the Maine property Carolyn left to Andy. Andy wanted to
be in control of the property and protect his privacy.

*April 14: He has brought the finished painting of "Ice Stream" to
show us. It's now a tempera. We just love it and he is proud.*

*April 16: Betsy is thrilled with "Ice Stream," but changes the name to
"Breakup."*

Andy related a story about gypsies in Chadds Ford. He was 14 when he
met a very pretty girl from the group. He showed her his toy collection. When
she left she kissed him on each cheek. She then cut off a lock of her hair and gave
it to him. "I will be back to marry you when you are old enough," she promised.
For years Andy kept the hair in a box waiting for her return.

May 11: Here we go! Cape May at 7 a.m. We go with Andy and

> *Betsy. Betsy takes a walk on the beach to collect shells. Andy is*
> *thrilled that Betsy is having such a good time. And truly she is!*
>
> *May 18: The new show is up at the museum. Andy is happy with the*
> *show. We must go see it.*
>
> *May 19: Andy talks about his education, art and family life. #1: Ten*
> *years ago was his best painting period. #2: His biggest mistake*
> *was going to Maine when he was young and not concentrating*
> *on his surroundings. #3: His father was a great teacher for him*
> *and Andy highly respected him. #4: He should have married a*
> *Chester County girl used to his area. #5: He worked very hard*
> *as a youngster on his art but he isolated himself at the same time*
> *as "the village idiot."*
>
> *May 21: George and I saw the new show yesterday. "Beauty Rest" was*
> *in it. We love it! May 27: We have a nice picnic. He'll be going*
> *to Maine next week. Death lurks with every move at his age (77*
> *this July) and his mind still wants to capture all that's available.*
> *He constantly plans for personal pleasure. He'll return in about*
> *a week.*
>
> *June 15: He called my office. He is not coming back until the fall.*
> *"You dirty dog!" I repeat again and again.*
>
> *July 21: Shock! He called my office. He held back purposely from*
> *calling. I knew it is spite for me. I'm too independent. He said*
> *he had "walking pneumonia." Maybe. George and I really do*
> *miss him.*

For the rest of the summer the phone calls from Andy were few and far between. Helen noted at times Andy seemed almost angry. He told Helen he planned on returning mid-October.

> *October 19: He sneaks in on us in the bedroom. We lavish him with*
> *attention and laughter. We show him Karl Kuerner's painting*
> *on loan of Andy. "That's me," he said. "Very interesting. Very*
> *good. How much does he want for it?" Andy did two paintings*
> *this summer, "Jupiter" and "Scuba."*
>
> *October 22: He invites us to the Mill to see his two new paintings.*
> *They are truly lovely. He is back to his old self again.*

*Note: Andy said he did "Jupiter" in just 2 and a half weeks. The girl
in the "Scuba" painting is Susan (a hired hand on the island.)*

*November 6: "Jupiter" is priced at $4,000,000. Andy asked if I
would like the $4,000,000 painting or him. I said him. He
laughed and admonished me severely. "My paintings ARE ME,"
he exclaims. "My work will talk when I'm gone," Andy said. I
agree and say I'd rather be talking to you now.*

*November 11: He is concerned about his prostate results. He is back
to his mortality thoughts again.*

November 18: He brings good news, no cancer. We're all delighted.

*November 28: He brought a picture of buzzards he's working on. He
bought a black casket. It will be delivered at 2 am some night in
secrecy. All is in preparation for the large death painting.*

Andy stopped by the Sipala home on Thanksgiving but didn't stay for a
long period. Helen believed Andy's Thanksgiving dinner was cancelled as his
sister Ann had a heart attack. Andy made sporadic visits before the Wyeth
Christmas party.

*December 17: A great spirited group! Jamie lost it completely and
tears streamed down his face with the Silent Night spoof. It was
a super evening and one we talked about for days. Jamie gave us
a signed print.*

December 21: Betsy got on the phone and raved about the party.

*December 24: Andy was in the kitchen wearing an apron cooking fish
for breakfast for us. Jamie delivered a fresh catch. What a sight!
He dips them in flour and fries in margarine.*

*December 27: George called Betsy. The show "Wyeth the Third
Generation" was on TV. She called Jamie.*

Chapter Seven
1995

Shocking Element

Andy had his first painting session of the year in the widow's walk during the middle of January. Andy was busy most days working with Frolic Weymouth on the purchase of the Kuerner property for the Brandywine Conservancy.

January 23: Frolic pulled out a check and said, "Go buy the
Kuerner's property at all costs. We must have it!" Andy told
Frolic, "Hold on, I'll work it."
January 24: Andy is going to talk to Kuerners today.
January 26: He brought over the painting of Johnny Testorf (Helga's
husband) for a preview. We really love it and we gush over the
model, colors and result. We play up our surprise of the model.
He kept the surprise from everyone, except Betsy, including
Helga. He thrives on the "shocking element." He wanted to hear
John's "other side of Helga's life." He didn't ask questions but let
Johnny open up. To his amazement, Johnny regrets not seeing
Helga more.

Andy wanted to confront Johnny before he died about Helga and make peace among the three of them. One of Andy's goals was to strengthen the relationship between Johnny and Helga. Andy believed Helga would be lonely and devastated after Andy's death. Andy was Helga's whole life, Helen concluded.

*January 26: Andy never promised to marry Helga and he would
never leave Betsy. I know Andy has promised Helga many other
things. Betsy now knows and likes Johnny and that makes Andy
feel good. It looks like Andy is tying up loose ends in lots of
matters as he ages. Helga was both thrilled and proud but also a
little disappointed and jealous with the painting. Her husband
got in her "territory."*

*February 2: We went to the Marshallton Inn. I tried to take him out
for privacy. There was only one other couple in the restaurant.
Surprisingly, he wanted to be noticed. He said hello loudly
from across the room to the strangers and spoke loudly of the
Wyeth family. I realized that attention fascinates him at times.
I'm trying to protect him and he is flaunting his presence. He
dresses so eccentric. He had on ski pants, a long green wool coat
(by Ralph Lauren designer), and huge light brown shoes with a
buckle. I'm slightly embarrassed by his appearance but, after all,
he is Andrew Wyeth!*

*February 4: Snow storm. Andy gets stuck at the bottom of our
driveway. George drives the car to the house. Andy was to buy
milk for Betsy. George put on Andy's coat and drove Andy's car
to get the milk and delivered it to Betsy. Many people waved at
George, thinking he was Andy.*

*February 15: We purchased a Cape Coat print and Andy offered to
sign it. We show him the prints "In the Orchard" and "Farm
Road" that he gave us. He said he was "honored" to have the
Helga paintings hanging in our house. Can you imagine?*

*February 21: He has been painting Hoarfrost. He won't tell us the
full story. We all have a good laugh guessing. He implies that it
is a woman.*

*March 5: Andy is in the widow's walk. Helga walks in without
knocking. George says, "You can't bother Andy, he's painting." She
proceeds upstairs. Andy tells her to leave. She comes down and
lingers awhile. I am furious and tell Andy so. Such an invasion of
privacy. She leaves in a hurry and runs over our flowerbeds.*

March 6: Andy told Helga we were angry and never to do that again.

John Liggett Meigs visited Andy for Ann Wyeth McCoy's 80th birthday celebration. Andy brought Meigs to see Painter's Folly and the Sipalas. Meigs was thinking about offering his art and book collection to the Brandywine River Museum. "An interesting man," Helen wrote. Meigs was a newspaper reporter and later involved in the art world. He is credited with designing the Hawaiian aloha shirts. He met artist Peter Hurd, husband of Henriette Wyeth, and was introduced to the Wyeth family.

Henriette visited Andy for Ann's birthday party and reported he was saddened at the state of Henriette's health.

Andy reported on a situation at the Farnsworth Museum in Maine where some of the collection might be discarded. The situation caused Andy to think about the disposition of his own paintings after his death.

March 25: Andy feared for his own collection in maybe 20 years. He came to work in the widow's walk. I was flabbergasted with the subject and progress. It's a scene of looking through the widow's walk window at the chimney, battlefield and church. I was so sincerely excited that he clearly was uplifted, inspired and delighted. "I need you," he said. "You give me spirit and vitality. You're fun to be around."

The Sipalas hosted a Spring dinner party for the Wyeth gang during early April. During dinner, Helen believed Betsy searched her home to see what paintings Andy had in the house. Helen wrote she didn't feel any warmth from Betsy and is distrustful.

About the same time Frolic Weymouth hosted a dinner where the guests were all prominent and wealthy people. A tipsy Frolic stood and gave a toast where he jokingly introduced George and Helen as: "The poorest people here." The guests all laughed at Frolic's teasing comments but Andy yelled at Frolic. "That's not nice! That's a terrible thing to say!" Helen interrupted and said, "But it's true!" George and Helen were not offended as Frolic was known for this type of antics and was a heavy drinker. Helen recorded, "A fabulous evening!"

Andy imparted a bit of sad news about the family; Phyllis Wyeth is in constant pain and thinks of her death. She has picked out the place she wants to be buried.

April 18: Helga called and talked to George. She feels she is keeping
Andy alive with her care and said he will die without it. Such
devotion and love Helga feels for Andy.

April 22: He came in very excited. We are invited to Maine. I protest
vehemently.

April 23: Andy joins me at church. Surprise! For the collection he
puts in $20 as his and my share. He thinks he is doing me a
favor. Much to the contrary, I did not feel good about this.
He dozes during the service. A group crowds around him
afterwards, shaking his hand. I tried to get him out quickly, to
no avail. I think he felt good about the whole experience.

May 4: His hip is bothering him and he will not get an operation.
He feels old. He is getting a cane but forgot it today. A new way
of life is pending for Andy, I can see. Doomsday haunts him in
the form of health. I give him a good back rub and he relishes it,
moaning and groaning with delight.

Andy invited Helen and George to see his new painting, *Moonlight*. "A
great painting of the widow's walk with a dome in the ceiling," Helen wrote.
Widow's walk doesn't have a dome. The idea came from a visit to Mt. Vernon
by Jamie. Jamie described a bull's eye dome and Betsy had a dream of floating
through this dome.

Andy received an art award in New York City and went by limo with
Carolyn, Victoria and Nicky. "They danced and had a wild time with the limo,"
Andy reported to Helen.

May 21: Andy came in with a cane. He's in a lot of pain. He is
planning to get some tests done. He doesn't want an operation.
He has a bad heart. His demeanor is depressed and quiet.

May 25: Betsy called to say Andy is in the hospital and is going to be
operated on tomorrow morning.

May 26: Betsy called again to report everything is fine with Andy.
She gave us a full report on the operation.

June 3: We called Andy at the hospital. He feels great. The bones were
deteriorating in the hip and the joint was worn down. It wore
out a long time ago. They meshed crushed bone around the hip

cavity and gave a new joint. His leg had atrophied and the hipbone was cracked. No wonder he had so much pain. He will need lots of therapy.

June 7: Andy is out of the hospital.

August 4: He calls and cancels our Maine trip. He is not in good health. He might have to have the other hip done. It was very disappointing.

October 2: Surprise. Andy called. He sounds chipper and feeling better. He invites us up for a weekend. I said it was too close to their coming home.

October 29: He's back. He looks great. We hug and tease him and he loves it.

November 4: I chided him privately about not calling for so long during the summer.

November 8: I really wish I had the time to scout around the hills with him. We have a lot in common. He makes me late for work. I will not have a Xmas party for the Wyeths this year. After this summer, I don't feel like it.

November 22: I think he is trying to find out if we are having a Xmas party. He brings up former guests and refers to the old parties here.

December 6: He surprises us. George puts on the Santa mask, red brief shorts and runs through the bedroom ringing Xmas bells.

December 17: George had been fretting all week thinking Andy and Betsy were mad at us because of no party. George drove me nuts about this. Today Andy shows up and George is happy.

December 31: He wanted to see us one more time before the New Year.

The beginning of another year with Andy —
the master of American art!

CHAPTER EIGHT
1996

Different type of perspective

January 1: He comes for a New Year's visit. We shared a few jokes,
had tea and he left. The beginning of another year with Andy —
the master of American art!

The year began with the completion of Andy's biography by Richard Meryman. Andy told Helen that Meryman had a falling out with Betsy. Meryman wanted Andy to read and approve the book and not have Betsy involved. Meryman had an unwelcomed request for Helen; Meryman wanted Helen to intercede to keep the book from Betsy.

January 6: Richard is writing a different type of perspective of
Andy – one more realistic, more artistic and by his description
should enhance his life and work, giving it an 'edge' as Andy
requested. Betsy has Andy stereotyped her way. Anyway that I
can help Richard will certainly be done very cautiously. I can't
side with Richard and alienate Andy. I won't tell Andy of our
conversations.
January 11: We had a terrible blizzard. He drew a picture of a silly
snowman (himself) and left it on the table.
January 12: Another snow storm.

> *January 14: We really missed him! Long time, no see! I hugged and*
> *hugged him and pampered him.*
> *January 29: We do miss him when he is not here for a week. Epps*
> *can't do anything about his eyes. Andy is getting old. That's all.*
> *He is doing a watercolor at the Mill but won't say who of.*

The month of February centered on the publication of the Meryman book.
Meryman communicated by letter with Andy through Helen.

> *February 21: I think Meryman was excellent in his messages. He had*
> *read this letter to me over the phone to get my opinion so as to*
> *not hurt his position with Andy and his book. I did advise him*
> *to be kind to Betsy in his letter as Andy is sensitive and in love*
> *with Betsy. He made some changes. Everyone involved is excited*
> *about the book. Andy gives these letters to us as Betsy must not*
> *see them.*
> *February 23: Another visit from Andy. He is enjoying the many*
> *snowstorms and has finished two paintings.*
> *February 25: He brings the painting of Gene E. du Pont Weymouth*
> *to show us. The painting is called "Blue Blood." It is very good*
> *and we are thrilled to be the first to see it. Betsy wants to send*
> *our painting of "Beauty Rest" to Baltimore to weave the two*
> *pieces together. I know she has a lot of interest in it, especially*
> *since the original was sold.*
> *February 28: Andy said Betsy changed the title of Gene Weymouth's*
> *painting of "Blue Blood" to his full name. We all think it is a*
> *better decision. Andy's book by Meryman will be called "The*
> *Secret Life of Andrew Wyeth." Very good!*
> *March 3: Andy put the ocean and boat in "The Widow's Walk" to*
> *represent the fateful trip of Howard Pyle to Europe. We talked a*
> *lot about Pyle today and his students.*

Meryman's relationship with Betsy continued to cause problems. A letter
to an editor at the *New Yorker* magazine by Meryman criticized Betsy's life with
Andy. "Where was Richard's head?" Helen wrote.

March 6: Betsy was angry with Meryman and Andy and flew into a range at Andy, as usual. Andy got up early this morning and fried potatoes and onions for Betsy as a form of peace offering. She softened only slightly and he left his house to come here. Andy said he wasn't afraid of bad publicity. "Whatever people say bad about me cannot be as bad as how I feel about myself. I am ashamed of myself and am constantly criticized. I am my own worst critic. I also have not been fair to you. I am nothing and I have nothing." I agree. Money and material things don't interest him nor does he get involved with them. He feels so inadequate, dejected, angry and beaten and seems to turn his attention to me for retaliation to Betsy. He is a beaten man. The conversation continues with George regarding Meryman's letter. I end the conversation by saying that Andy will have to fix potatoes and onions for a few more days. We all laugh.

During another March conversation Andy went through his book and identified models and told stories of various paintings.

○ *Roasted Chestnuts* is Allen Messermit

○ *Spring Wind* is James Lopez. He is buried in Potter's Field cemetery at Embreeville State Hospital. We looked for his grave.

○ *Winter* is Allen Lynch

○ *Snow Flurries* is the hill above Archie's Church in Chadds Ford.

○ *Garret Room* is Tom Clark. When he died, a relative told Andy they would need more money to buy him a bigger casket, as he was so tall. Andy told her to take his shoes off. "What a great idea, we'll do that," she said. Andy still laughs about it.

○ *Monologue* is Willard Snowden.

○ *The Drifter* is Willard Snowden. He had been drinking and Andy painted a bit of wine on his lips. He sat up close to Andy, completely absorbed in Andy's brushes. That was when Andy was prompted to paint him on the spot. Willard fell forward into Andy's lap with an epileptic fit. It shocked Andy but Andy had instructions to put something in his mouth to prevent injury. Andy placed a pencil between Willard's teeth.

○ *Granddaughter* is Cathy Hunt, granddaughter of Alexander Chandler.

○ *Day of the Fair* is Cathy Hunt. She is all dressed up for the Chadds Ford fair. Her pensive, uneasy look was the result of posing so long. When Andy asked what was wrong, she said, "Today's the fair." She was anxious to leave.

○ *Monday Morning* – Betsy left her clothes basket out and it snowed in it leaving the clothes pins slightly exposed.

○ *Toll Rope* – Andy was in the belfry when a funeral began. He was stuck there for about two hours until it was over. At times the bell would ring in his ears. He didn't dare move as the door to the belfry was over the congregation.

○ *The Sexton* is Wayne Mattson.

○ *Perpetual Care* is the rear of Wyle Corner Church, Maine. Andy was busy painting and people were patiently standing by. He asked them to leave. "We only want to place flowers on the grave," they said. Andy was totally embarrassed and apologized. Hence the flowers in the picture.

April 21: He comes for a favor. Meryman is coming to town and
    Betsy doesn't want to see him. Would we entertain him? Of
    course I volunteer before he had the chance to get out the words.

April 25: Connie and Mike were in from Michigan (my brother
    Cliff's friends). She is a Wyeth 'nut.' They got to meet Andy. She
    burst into tears with surprise and delight. Andy is so gracious
    and delightful with people. Meryman went back to N.Y. and
    didn't come over. Dolly Parker entertained him.

May 3: Andy gets Meryman's letters and allows us to read them.
    He doesn't want Betsy to know of this secret correspondence in
    preparation for the book.

May 12: Andy told us Bill Gates bought "Distant Thunder" from the
    Woolworth family for a high sum. Mrs. Woolworth flew with the
    painting to a destination and Gates made a surprise entrance
    and astounded even a Woolworth! The price can't be discussed by
    the Woolworths.

Andy had a different type of request for Helen. Andy required "course white flour" for a painting and Helen looked for a mill that had the essential item. For the painting, Andy wanted authentic flour. A trip was made to the Nolt mill in Bird-in-Hand, Pennsylvania. Andy took three antique flour bags to be filled, but one had a hole in it.

> *May 22: He comes with his new painting "Plundered" of the flour,*
> *mill and soldiers. The soldiers are covering their white leggings*
> *with flour to clean them. He said you can just hear the soldiers*
> *in the upper windows yelling, "What the f. are you doing down*
> *there?" He feels the crudeness and rudeness of the pilfering as it*
> *was historically recorded. It is his mill and he feels it personally.*
> *He threw the flour all over the ground and Knome, the dog, kept*
> *licking it up as he was painting. No one posed and uniforms*
> *and flags were researched. He drew the mill as it was back then.*
> *It was a really delightful painting and quite a change for him.*
> *May 25: Andy brings us a 10 lb. bag of the mill flour.*

Andy wanted edits to the Meryman book, especially about Helga. Helen and Andy attempted to reach Meryman but couldn't do so.

> *May 26: Andy is concerned about Meryman. I call Meryman and*
> *Andy talks to him. "It's just not important to mention Helga,"*
> *he reasons. "A typical "Life" magazine move to titillate the*
> *public." Andy tells Meryman, "Don't read me anymore, just do*
> *it. I don't want to read the book and I don't want to take the*
> *edge out of it."*
> *May 27: Memorial Day 8 a.m. He is here again. He surely must be*
> *preparing to leave for Maine. He is very attentive today and says,*
> *"You'll always be my friend, remember that!" When we come*
> *downstairs George had prepared a Memorial Day decoration*
> *on the kitchen table: flags, 3 guns, flowers, a funeral urn and a*
> *funny statement for us to read. He has Sousa marches playing.*
> *We dance around the kitchen, carrying the flag. He takes us*
> *down to the Mill to show us "Artic Circle" of Mary Landa.*
> *May 29: Andy called and invited us to Maine. Betsy also got on the*
> *phone. We agreed to visit at the end of July.*

Helen and George visited Maine from July 25 through July 28. Despite rainy weather, the Sipalas and Andy walked the island. On one outing, Andy said he was concerned for Betsy after the Meryman book is released. "Wait and see how many people dislike her. She'll be shocked. I don't want to be around when it comes out."

The Sipalas had little recorded contact with Andy until he returned in October. The couple hosted a party in November where Betsy wanted Frank Fowler to attend and Helen did not. Fowler didn't. Andy was very angry because Betsy didn't get her way, Helen wrote. Helen added about the party, "What a sight to see the wealthy brown nosing the wealthy!"

Helen reported the Wyeths and Meryman were on good terms since the book seemed to be selling. Meryman was busy with interviews on television shows and book signings.

> *November 20: He brought the "N.Y. Times'" article on his book. It was a good review and made for good conversation. He was proud of it.*
>
> *November 21: Betsy is working out a deal with Bill Gates: trade her computer copy system on her paintings for building a museum in Maine at the Olson property and purchasing "Christina's World" for the Farnsworth Museum. This is TOP secret, as nothing is finalized. He and Betsy, especially Betsy, are very excited about this. We don't dare tell.*
>
> *November 30: We haven't seen him for about a week. It seems like a long time. He had a bad cold.*
>
> *December 12: Meryman is trying desperately to get Andy to have an interview with the "New York Times." Andy keeps getting our opinion about the whole mess. There are lots of pros and cons. He wants to help Meryman with the book but detests chancing an interview.*

As Helen and George decorated for the holidays, Nicky mentioned that Andy especially likes visiting them at Christmas. Andy missed having a decorated home. Helen and George hosted the Christmas party for the Wyeths on December 14 with Andy, Betsy and a half dozen other guests attending, including Meryman.

> *December 18: Andy agreed to do the interview with Meryman. Andy came to thank us for the great party.*
>
> *December 20: Andy, Helga, Jamie, Nicky and Victoria popped in unexpectedly. They stopped to see the decorated house that the Wyeths raved about.*

CHAPTER NINE
1997

Andy receives a "rousing welcome"

Helen and George greeted Andy with "Happy New Year" as he entered Painter's Folly during the morning of January 1. Helen thanked Andy for all of the "nice things" he did for them during the year and specifically mentioned Andy's laughter, jokes and visits. The Sipalas had bad news to share, George lost his job. Andy offered to give the couple signed prints and books to sell. "It was very generous of him and thoughtful," Helen noted.

January 30: I was sick with a cold but had tea with George and
Andy. He told us about a new painting called "The Guest
Room." It is a black girl who posed in small pigtails. He and
Betsy dressed her in Betsy's clothes. She posed in Wyeth's house.
He is excited about the painting.

Note: I got busy and lazy with writing so I forgot particulars (of first
three weeks of February.)

February 21: Meryman called this am. He wants Andy to agree to a
show at the Whitney Museum. Meryman has entrusted me with
secrecy. I am to encourage Andy only if he brings up the subject.
I'm not really crazy about such influence asked of me. I don't
like such secrecy.

February 25: He brought the painting "Night Sleeper" over to us. I

> *wasn't home.*
>
> *March 6: I asked Andy to speak at my women's club or just make an*
> *appearance. He didn't like the idea at all. It was a mistake in*
> *asking him.*
>
> *March 20: He had been sick with spitting up blood again.*
>
> *March 27: The Whitney Museum curator and administrator are*
> *coming to visit the Wyeths. They want a show. Wyeths are still*
> *resentful that Whitney was only showing art deco material and*
> *ignored the more traditional art for many years.*

The death of Henriette in April coincided with Andy slowing his visits to Painter's Folly.

> *May 8: Andy made a remark on "Master Bedroom" for us. This*
> *should be valuable, as he has never done one before expect one*
> *for a family member.*

On May 15, Andy's wedding anniversary, Andy was acting like a "mean and cruel person." George had killed a raccoon causing a mess at Painter's Folly. That incident started a conversation. The dialogue switched to the death of Betsy's dog, and a murder case gaining national attention. "We should be killing more people instead of animals. Animals are better," Andy said.

Andy then turned to religion and the role of women in the world. He condemned all who went to church, calling them hypocrites and do-gooders. "They think they are perfect," he said. As for women, he said they were "dominant and cruel." Helen wrote, "Today is not a good day and the visit is strange and edgy, even though Andy smiles through it all. His visit did not sit well with me. I found it very upsetting all day. There was too much bitterness coming from a person who is known to be calm and gentle."

> *May 19: Andy brings a sketch of the recent painting he is working*
> *on. It is of "Senna," a black girl working for Frolic. She has*
> *fair skin and a nice body. He is painting her nude in a running*
> *position. It really is quite good and the idea is both new for*
> *Andy and a great change of pace. He is going to put the comet*
> *Hale Bobb in the sky. He visited a museum to view the comet.*

> *The painting will be quite large. It was quite a privilege for us
> to see it. A practice that Andy rarely does for anyone else.*
> *May 24: He is concerned about the sale at Sotheby's. (Earlier Helen
> wrote that he and Betsy seem to be placing his life's work on
> this sale because it might determine the market value later.) He
> mentions it every time he comes. I was still feeling the effects of
> the May 15 visit. Andy isn't as attentive as he was before. Is it
> my imagination? I think he is being entertained and busy with
> a new model (Senna Moore) and directs his attention elsewhere.
> He has been giving her money and he and Frolic will put her
> through school. It is a great idea!*
> *May 27: Channel 10 carried the story on Meryman's book. The
> painting "Marriage" was shown.*
> *May 31: Andy comes while Sister Loretta is visiting. Andy bought a
> handmade $30 silver cross from Loretta and she was flattered.
> Andy brought George a watercolor. It is called "Wild Rose
> Hips." He is on an upbeat now, even though it is nearing
> departure time. They are late in leaving for Maine. He recently
> gave us two new prints ("Harlequin" and "Southern Comfort"
> which were artist's proofs #1.) How generous of him.*

During Andy's summer in Maine he called a few times to talk about his paintings and to say he might have another hip replacement. He also indicated he wouldn't be home until after Halloween, a late return for the Wyeths.

Helen gave Andy a "rousing welcome" upon his return. Helen believed Andy was embarrassed for not inviting them to Maine that summer. Helen wrote she had no desire to visit them again.

> *November 6: He signs the painting of the vultures for us. This was a
> gift many years ago but left in one of our closets for several years.
> He had asked about it and I brought it out and showed him.
> He said, "You people have no idea what you have." After that
> we had it framed and hung it in the house. He was delighted
> that we still had it. We were never excited about it but thought
> we should have him sign it before something happens to him.
> This watercolor was done when Andy was in one of his "death*

moods." This period lasted most of one year.

*November 7: He stopped in and removed a watercolor, "Rose Hips,"
that he finished.*

*November 15: He is wearing another pair of Betsy's pants. He looks
outrageous! We talk about the new museum in Rockland, Nicky's
life, the Brandywine museum and the Kuerners. He tried to
convince Karl to paint his mother in bed while she is sick.
He promised a sketch for Karl if he accomplished this but the
mother threatened to leave him out of her will. I see Andy uses a
cane now.*

*November 16: Andy invites us to see his new paintings: "Omen,"
"Privy" and "Winter Fodder." We joked and laughed about the
nude paintings.*

*November 27: Jamie is invited to do a portrait of Pres and Mrs.
Clinton. This is quite an honor.*

*December 2: Mrs. Anna Kuerner was buried today at the
Brandywine Baptist Church. I went and Andy spoke at the
service. Anna is gone now. The last of the Kuerner's Hill couple
and the last of a big part of Andy's life.*

The Wyeths' Christmas party was held on December 13 with Andy and
Betsy attending. The special guest was Phyllis Diller. Helen read that Diller was
at the Exton Mall for her art show and she gave Diller an invitation. During the
party, George unveiled Stan Zukin's restored N. C. Wyeth painting of World
War II. Helen called the party a "very dramatic event!"

December 14: He comes eager to rehash the wonderful party.

*December 15: Andy put a remark on the painting "Marsh Hawk" for
us.*

*December 17: Betsy wants to know how I got Diller. Did I use
(Betsy's) influence? I call. She asks about Diller but I tell little
and change the subject. Betsy talks for a long time about the
fabulous "magical" party. She said she and Andy "felt like they
were to a show and went to bed with smiles on their faces."*

*December 25: All the family is here and Andy stops in. We greet him
warmly but thank goodness he doesn't stay long.*

Chapter Ten
1998

Andy enchants Phyllis Diller

The year began with Helen receiving a letter from Phyllis Diller thanking Helen for the invitation to the Wyeths' Christmas party. "You and your husband have created the most gorgeous warm haven in that beautiful home," Diller wrote. "I'm totally enchanted with Andrew and Betsy … Your dinner was one of the high points of our lives."

Phyllis added a post script inviting Helen and George to be entertained at her California home.

Andy made frequent visits to see the Sipalas in January but didn't work at Painter's Folly. Andy had a bad cold for part of the month. Helen wrote, "We keep our distance. He looks tired and miserable."

February 12: He tried to stay away with his cold but is feeling better.
He is getting his hand operated on next Tuesday and wanted
us to know. The hand had been hurting and full of growths,
making painting difficult. He is fearful that he may have
permanent damage.
February 16: He makes one last stop before his operation tomorrow.
He is using Dr. Coggins from Wilmington and is very confident
in him.
February 19: Andy is back. The hand is lightly bandaged and
the doctor said, "Use it." He went to St. Francis Hospital as

an outpatient, was given a sedative and the hand was only numbed. He was able to watch the operation. So unlike the other operations: no hospital stay, no therapy no pain, no excess bandaging and Andy is happy as a lark! Both hands experienced growths on the muscles and tendons, which pulled his hand closed. Since this was his painting hand, he was dubious about the operation and the doctor teased that his own reputation was at stake during the procedure.

February 23: He is eager to show us the partially exposed hand. The large bandage is off and Andy is back to painting. He is given a special glove to keep it clean while working. Andy is happy. George gives him some ointment for some stress in his wrist that might be arthritis. They laugh about "Dr. George."

February 26: The bandage is off.

Andy, Betsy and the Sipalas exchanged Valentine gifts and later Easter gifts. During one visit Andy discloses "so much confidential information," according to Helen. Andy told them of Jamie selling a large painting and Frank Fowler's trip to Japan for an art deal. Andy also said he is dismayed and disappointed with talks about him purchasing the Kuerner estate as the comment was made that Andy had made a lot of money off the paintings featuring the Kuerners. The estate was eventually purchased by Frolic Weymouth and the Brandywine Conservancy.

February 28: Here he comes in a hunting coat that belonged to Peter Hurd (circa 1930s). It is red with an orange collar and brass buttons with initials. The coat is exceptionally dirty, of good quality and heavy. Henriette's family sent him several of Peter's coats. He is so proud of this coat but I don't see how Betsy could let him leave the house with it on. I hope he gets it cleaned. He, with black tights, large black sneakers and his long red riding coat, is a sight to behold. He makes himself eccentric, like most artists.

Helen entertained Victoria, Andy's granddaughter, on her 19th birthday with a breakfast feast. Helen wrote, "We had a great time and Victoria was surprised, appreciative and thrilled with it all. Andy and Nicky were pleased. We tooted the horns and sang happy birthday. Fun, Fun!" The Sipalas were also invited to Maine for the opening of a new show, Wondrous Strange.

April 23: There was a sale at Stuart Kingston's of one of Andy's paintings. Andy is very curious. George investigates for him.

May 1: May Day! Here he comes with a basket of wild flowers, wine for George and a signed print of "Master Bedroom." I jump up and down with joy!

May 2: Andy takes George and me to his father's studio. There was a large group of guides from a museum in Philadelphia taking a tour. The three of us march right in and Andy by-passes the security ropes and takes us right down into the heart of the studio. Everyone tries to remain quiet and tactfully ignore us. It was a privileged experience for us.

May 3: He takes me to Kuerners to see the buttercups and I drive his car. We walk on the hill a little and sit in the car and enjoy the view. He offers me any financial help I might ever need and promises me more paintings to support me when I'm old. Can you imagine this! Our lives have a lot in common and we always compare them.

May 7: He is coming more frequently. I bet he is getting ready for Maine. He is probably slowing down on his paintings and killing more time.

May 21: Our weekly Thursday visit. He tells us of the new painting he finished. It is of Messersmith ... the man who posed for "Roasted Chestnuts." It is a fascinating and wonderful painting, one of those strange faces with unusual country attire. He made me cover my eyes while George was taking it out of the trunk. We jump out of our skin with delight with the painting. We could see he was thrilled with our response.

Helen and George received an invitation to attend an art show at the Whitney Museum of American Art in New York City. They attended and later wrote a thank you to the Wyeths for arranging the invitation. Andy, by this time, was in Maine.

On June 19, Helen and George traveled to Maine for the opening of the Wondrous Strange show at the Farnsworth Art Museum in Rockland. They stayed for four days. Betsy arranged a tour of the museum for the Sipalas. During the summer and early fall, Andy made periodic calls to the couple.

After Andy returned to Chadds Ford, a bus load of 17 people from the Greenville County Museum of Art in South Carolina toured Painter's Folly. Andy specially requested Helen and George to be hosts for the group. Helen suggested Andy join them on the bus tour, but he declined. When the tour arrived, Andy was on the front porch to greet the group. "Can you imagine the shock, delight and thrill of seeing the artist in person?" Helen wrote. "We were all ecstatic beyond words!"

The South Carolina museum was in negotiations with the Wyeths to purchase another one of Andy's paintings. Betsy was especially appreciative of the hospitality displayed by Helen and George.

> *November 7: We discuss politics, Michaelis's book (David Michaelis wrote "N. C. Wyeth"). Ann did not like the book, especially because it did not include much about her husband, John McCoy. I asked Andy if he would mind a book revealing ALL about him. He said he wouldn't give a shit. He felt the book about his father was well written and complete.*
>
> *November 13: Today we questioned him at length about the book "N.C. Wyeth." I asked him which museum he felt closer to (Farnsworth or Brandywine) and he said Brandywine, even though he and Betsy contributed a lot to both.*

Helen questioned Andy about his thoughts on depression, insecurity, wealth and his relationship with his surroundings and African Americans. Andy said he wasn't interested in wealth. He insisted only his sister Carolyn suffered from depression. "He always knew he was different and closer to his surroundings," Helen wrote. "He always avoided social situations when young and preferred the company of his black friend, DoDo, or the quiet of the hills." Andy loved rehashing the book's passages of his early days. The conversation continued.

> *November 13: Were you as critical of yourself as your father? "God,*

*no! If I did something good that was fine with me, period.
Even now, I really don't care if I am successful in a painting or
not. The pressure is not there. Betsy has been good for me and
we have a good marriage, but she was the overall best choice
in my case. I came from Chadds Ford, the country and Betsy
was from Maine, the islands and water and we have each kept
to our own roots. She wanted to win me over and gets angry
that I never changed." Regarding N. C. Wyeth and sister-in-
law Carolyn: He believed they had a love affair even though
Betsy doesn't believe it. Knowing the secrets that Andy told me
years ago, I firmly believe it too. He said that Carolyn was a
beautiful woman and his father would have been a fool to do
so otherwise. Andy revealed many stories to George and I. One
of the most embarrassing and low periods of Andy's artistic
life was surpassing his father and watching his father sink
in spirit. Howard Pyle took advantage of N. C. and then N.
C. took advantage of his students – repeating an unpleasant
cruelty or relationship. He pushed and punished, ridiculed and
challenged, loved and hated the very ones closest to him in the
art world. They affected him and in turn he affected them – very
much identical to Howard Pyle. This was his teaching.*

The day's intense conversation concluded with a discussion of invitations
for the upcoming Christmas party and a clash between Betsy and Steve Bruni,
head of the Delaware Art Museum. The play *Wondrous Strange* was scheduled
to be shown at the museum and Bruni wasn't listening to suggestions by Betsy
for the staging. Finally the museum's board intervened and Betsy prevailed.
"Betsy wins BIG again!" Helen wrote.

*November 20: We invite Andy and Helga to join us for lunch in West
Chester. Andy and Helga's relationship would surprise anyone.
Andy said that some people hate to have her around because of
her bazaar appearance. What the heck, Andy says, I like her
that way. It's natural – not fake. In the restaurant she feeds him
like a patient and spouse all in one. He allows it and perhaps
has grown to depend on her like a child. We see Stan Zukin*

(Helen's employer) and Stan asks permission to take pictures. I could see that Andy was hesitant and with a word from me he turned them down. I could just see Betsy seeing this picture and Andy getting in trouble. Andy's travels are usually private. Andy is sponsoring a film on his sister Ann that should cost about $200,000. Her son will do it. Andy swore us to secrecy. He wants to do this for her.

November 26: Andy, Victoria and Nicky dropped in. Victoria had a serious hangover from the night out on the town with Frolic and some friends.

November 28: The trio visit us again and invited us to breakfast at the Chadds Ford Café. When we entered, Victoria made it extremely obvious that they were the Wyeths. She was so loud at the table that the whole place could hear her. George and I could have crawled under the table. Nothing could keep her quiet. Andy kept yelling out loud, "I'm glad you took down all those old Wyeth paintings." The restaurant's décor had changed to Florida colors and decorations. He was obviously disturbed with the change in a Chadds Ford local restaurant, one without his signature. This shocked us as he usually likes to be ignored and have lots of privacy (or does he ????) George and I were mortified.

December 2: He sneaked up the stairs and surprised George and me in bed again. Its been a long time since he did that. I don't think he likes climbing the stairs.

December 10: Ann called to confirm our party date.

The annual Christmas party took place on December 12. Helen reported Betsy was "glued" to Charles Cawley and ignored the woman on her left. "I must remember to put a man on each side of Betsy in the future," Helen noted. Charles Michael Cawley was a founding member of the bank MBNA.

December 13: Betsy said, "Who could they have next, the President?" Betsy was very ecstatic.

December 14: Cawley called Jamie to say the party was a blast! Cawley commented, "I think I replaced Phyllis Diller." Andy was pleased with the party.

December 26: Cawley called Jamie and asked to visit the museum. Cawley promised a donation of one million immediately and one million every year for three years. We can't help but feel that our cozy dinner party enhanced the Wyeths' relationship with Cawley.

The Sipalas ended the year with a week in Florida.

CHAPTER ELEVEN
1999

Andy Paints Victoria

The last year of the century began with frequent visits and conversation about family, neighbors and friends. Andy helped the Sipalas by signing a letter protesting the possible taking of land owned by the couple for the expansion of Route 1. The road runs along the front of Painter's Folly. Eventually the Pennsylvania Department of Transportation took less of the Sipalas' land than first requested. Charles Crawley and his attorney also greatly aided the effort.

January 28: He shows us a copy of a "Look" magazine picture of him holding one of his paintings in a burned out field near his studio. Nicky is flying a miniature airplane and caught the field on fire. Fire engines were called but a good portion of the field was burned. A great story.

February 9: George and I went to the opening of the "Wondrous Strange" play at the Delaware Art Museum. Mary Landa and Helga were there. It was terrific!

February 11: Betsy, Andy, Frolic, Helga and others saw the play and all loved it. The good word is spreading and the play was sold out for the rest of the period. Maybe it will go to Maine and/or Chadds Ford through Frolic.

February 12: Helga took the cast of the play out to dinner and gave them signed Helga books.

*February 28: Phyllis Wyeth is in poor condition in a Maine hospital.
She has pneumonia and other problems since she recently fell.*
*March 7: It is a bitter cold morning. He loves to rehash the beginning
of our friendship and the many things we did together. He is
very sentimental and flirts a lot. He loves to tease. He feels young
and rejuvenated by being here. He asks if I am writing any of
it down. "You should," he says. I don't want him to know that I
am most of the time.*
*March 13: He had to attend a meeting at the Sanderson Museum as
he is on the board. He doesn't relish that type of meeting. It's sort
of out of his line.*

The Wyeths' bookkeeper, Peter Ray, died from an epileptic seizure. His death was a shock. The evening of his passing, two of Peter's relatives were found in Peter's office rummaging through papers. Betsy sent Andy to investigate. They were looking for Peter's insurance papers, or so they said. Andy helped them look and made them leave. Later it was determined that Peter's office was in good order, satisfying the Wyeths.

A Wyeth account with funds was found to be missing. Andy told Peter's son that if he finds these funds he would split them with him. Helen wrote, "These funds might be an eternal secret. This case has caused uproar in many ways and Betsy is determined to get to the bottom of it."

*April 15: Phyllis Wyeth is still not well and has changed hospitals.
Staph infection. Frolic is looking a little better and getting
around slowly.*
*April 22: He has a bruised and drooping eyelid, a scratch on the head
and a bruise on his leg. He was jumping across a small stream,
the rock moved and he fell in the water. He was quite angry
with himself and we teased him a lot.*

For May Day, Helen and George composed a little poem to go along with their gifts for Andy and Betsy. The main piece was a basket sculpture depicting Kuerner's hill from a hump and covered with sod with a tree and flowers. Helen wrote that it was hard to describe. Helen and George did get a laugh from their efforts at creating a sculpture.

Dear Betsy & Andy:
Now, what to give on May Day
Our thoughts did go astray.
For why a bunch of posies
When our minds would like to play.

We'll duplicate a painting
As goofy as it looks.
Maybe Braids, Raccoon or Souring
But not like in the books.

Ah! We think we have a good one
That's bound to bring delight.
We tried to make a Kuerner's Hill
Did you guess it right?

Happy May Day!

May 16: Andy is painting Brip du Pont's daughter. She is a student in New York and he gave her a hundred dollars for posing. He was surprised that she was so grateful. Has he forgotten the needs of young people? Besides, she was paying for her train ticket. He is doing her nude by the Brandywine. He asked her to disrobe but if she felt uncomfortable he would get someone else to pose for the nudity. That's his "carrot" because she immediately agreed to do it. He is a winner in this category.

May 24: We all hug a lot and I detect no joy in his trip to Maine. Maybe he questions his mortality. It's all rather sad but we send him off. I find his emotional side most endearing.

During Andy's sojourn to Maine, he called several times. Andy was concerned about George's health.

August 12: He is painting Victoria and getting great results. He is very talkative today and in high spirits.

September 8: We leave for Maine with the Hartnesses and return on the 12th. Betsy drove us all around the island in a golf cart. She has cleared a lot of the island to reveal an abundance of wild ferns and evergreens. On one end of the island is a turbulent current with a dramatic drop in rock formation. They have a future graveyard that is encircled in small rocks and resembling a garden. It is here that Betsy says a plaque will state: "This is where angels fear to tread because here lies Betsy and Andy dead."

October 1: He called. Charles Cawley bought one of his paintings of Victoria. One of the paintings looked a little too sexy and Cawley did not feel it would show well in his professional surroundings.

October 28: He's back. He looks terrific and says the same for us.

October 29: He bought a Halloween mask for George to put together for him (a skeleton with "blood" running down it & operated by a hand pump.) Great idea and given by Victoria.

November 2: His sister, Ann, shared a copy of a letter that was sent to Henriette by a writer describing N. C. Wyeth's funeral, as Henriette couldn't attend because of a tough pregnancy. His description of the letter brought tears to my eyes. The letter described the funeral in minute detail and was about ten pages long. Will be made public someday, I'm sure.

November 3: George comes across a painting for sale and told Andy. It is one of the studies for "Tracks." He thinks it is selling too cheaply and considers buying it for Betsy for Xmas. Jean Wyeth finally got married and Andy and Betsy were puzzled by her wedding announcement: "Mrs. Nathaniel Wyeth marries so and so. They thought it was in bad taste. She should have used HER name, not her deceased husband's.

November 5: There is going to be a Black Wyeth art show in Tennessee. Betsy is doing the footnotes for the pictures and everyone is very excited about it. Andy is curious about the turnout.

A business deal where George attempted to sell a Wyeth painting for Frank Fowler through Lee Conklin and Discount Framing ended badly with George not being compensated. When the painting arrived, the frame was slightly dam-aged and Fowler "hit the roof" and complained to Andy. George was involved in several calls to "smooth" over the difficulty.

> *November 10: George explains what REALLY happened. Fowler blew*
> *it all out of proportion. Fowler's secretary innocently revealed*
> *a different version of the damage. We realized Fowler saw an*
> *opportunity to discredit everyone to his favor. There has always*
> *been a jealous side of Fowler when it came to Andy's work.*
>
> *November 13: Everyone is pleased with Erin Smith's handling of*
> *the new art show in the Farnsworth Museum in Maine. Betsy*
> *invited her to be on the Board at the museum. Andy painted a*
> *portrait of Erin.*
>
> *November 16: Andy asks George if he should make prints of one of*
> *his paintings for the benefit and upkeep of the Kuerner property.*
> *Frolic, and others, want to place it on the Internet. Andy feels*
> *Betsy will veto it as it cheapens them. "We must keep our*
> *dignity," said Andy. George and I both felt there was no harm.*

Just before Thanksgiving Andy reported on the health of his family. Nicky was doing well after his operation but still has a lot pain.

> *November 17: He shows us cards that Victoria sent him. The*
> *envelopes are always covered with funny and colorful stamps.*
> *He said he offered Victoria one of his paintings if she would stop*
> *smoking and using "that crazy stuff for her head." He said she*
> *obviously didn't care as he ended up selling the painting. He is*
> *visiting more often than usual this year and I'm not sure why.*
> *Maybe it is because I'm retired and at home all day.*
>
> *November 20: Today he tells us about a hollow tree he is painting and*
> *his excitement is obvious.*
>
> *November 28: Nicky nearly died from clogged arteries and kidney*
> *failure resulting from the double hip replacement. Jamie rushed*
> *to be with him in Maine. Wyeths were very concerned.*
>
> *December 2: Nicky is coming along OK and should be home soon.*

The Wyeths' Christmas party took place on December 4. The entertainment was a belly dancer. Helen wrote a long letter to Phyllis Diller describing the party and enclosed a photo of the dancer. Helen recorded, "In this group we had the person who bought "Marriage." He spent the weekend with us and we let him sleep in the Marriage bed. The second "surprise" was a couple from N. Carolina who owned more than 150 Wyeth paintings." She mentioned Tony Bennett had considered joining them but decided against attending.

> *December 12: Andy and Helga delivered an original study of "Marriage" to us for a Christmas present. He said he "brought us a print." When I tore an opening in the paper and saw a study of Marriage I went into shock! Not a print but the real McCoy! I started crying with disbelief and shock. He told me privately that I've done so many nice things for others that I deserve something for myself. I'm sure he meant George and I and was referring to our hospitality. It was his way of saying thanks. Little does he know how he has enriched our lives. What a day in our lives – one memorable day!!*
>
> *December 18: Brip du Pont donated $100,000 for the upkeep of the Kuerner property, quite a donation! Nicky is slowly getting better. Still in the hospital.*
>
> *December 30: Another visit. He seems to be here almost every other day. We wish him a Happy New Year!*

*He visits no one else on a regular basis and
hopes to never wear out his welcome.*

CHAPTER TWELVE
2000

Last conversation with N. C. Wyeth

The new millennia began with a scare for both the Sipalas and Helga. Andy had not been seen for almost a week and all were concerned.

January 5: We find out that he had been sick with a cold. For some reason, he feels guilty if he hasn't been here for a few days. Is it because he enjoys the visit so much or does he feel obligated or does he think we will worry about him ??? I'm inclined to think he misses the chance to relax privately away from Betsy and Helga.

January 8: He has no appetite or energy. Still getting over his illness. He is concerned about one woman becoming too attached. He has gotten himself in a sticky situation (originally his fault) and now is hounded by her. His ego and temptation are not dead at the age of 82 and now he is running scared with the results. My how the men do talk! A traditional male problem! If these women only knew! He and Jamie share this problem and enjoy each other's comfort and titillations. A family tradition.

January 18: Odd Nerdrum, an artist from Norway, was in Philadelphia. And was invited to visit the Wyeths. Andy said Betsy found him very interesting, both in character and

*appearance. Nerdrum complimented Andy's work so that
endeared the Wyeths.*

*January 27: He tells us of a portrait he painted of him and a girl
having sex. He says it is in a vault. He said it is the size of
"Night Sleeper." We tease him about Betsy's reaction. He said he
will be dead then and won't give a damn. This is a story that he
has repeated before, so I guess it is might be true. He is not only
devilish but over-sexed as well!*

Andy's attention turned to Nicky, who is not healing and was scheduled
to repeat the two operations on his hips. The Wyeth family was concerned but
Nicky remained upbeat and philosophical about the situation.

For Valentine's Day, Andy gave Betsy his painting *Scuba*. Helen wrapped
the gift. For additional presents, Andy asked the Sipalas to purchase five copies
of the book *Girl with a Pearl Earring*. Helen and George were to receive one.
Andy believed the story, in a way, was about Helga. The other four copies were
to go to Andy's sister, Helga, Jamie and Nicky. Later, Andy increased the book
order to seven copies.

*NOTE: I read the "Girl with a Pearl Earring" and can see why he
is so fascinated and anxious for others to read it. It's about a
famous artist (Andy?), a maidservant (Helga?) and an over-
powering wife (Betsy?). Betsy could "see" Helga but I wonder if
she could "see" herself in this book.*

*February 13: He got a letter from a man in prison who wanted to
correspond with him. This fellow had all kinds of problems.
This seems to be the case with celebrity mail but the Wyeths just
laugh it off.*

February 14: Betsy loved the painting "Scuba."

*February 17: Today it snowed and he loves to venture out. He drives
through my flower gardens in the snow and even ran over a
small wire fence and rocks. He broke the window on the side of
his truck with a tree branch. Reckless or old? The truck is loaded
with dents and scratches.*

February 25: It has been almost a week since we saw him. He has been working double duty on a painting. He says Betsy won't like it or at least will be shocked with it. It must be a woman, nude, or exotic subject matter. He mentions Nicky might not need the operations. A doctor friend asked Andy to autograph Andy's book so that the doctor could take it to Washington to visit President Clinton. Andy wrote something to the effect "you are doing a good job." Now Andy is excited that Clinton might write to him or invite him to the White House for a visit.

Helen and George joined Andy and Helga for a disastrous lunch. Helen wrote that she didn't believe what she saw and heard. Andy spilled sugar and papers on the table, talked in a loud voice and dropped his utensils. Helga was worse, as she washed each piece of her wings in water because she believed they were too spicy. Helga had barbecue sauce all over her and then hand-fed Andy. "George and I are embarrassed," Helen noted.

During the ride home from the restaurant, Helga drove so slowly that a line of cars with irritated drivers paraded behind her. She crossed the middle line while sightseeing and stopped to take photographs of nothing obvious, Helen reported. "Andy & Helga consider the lunch date as a great time," Helen noted.

March 8: He wants to know what we thought of our trip with Helga. We talk about the good meal and the good time we had. He laughs and reminds us that she is a foreigner. We don't bite. In truth, he would not want us to speak ill of her and we don't.

March 10: He tells us about Frolic going to New York to meet Prince Philip.

March 17: He is still thrilled with the prospect of going to Washington to see Pres. Clinton. He heard through the grapevine that Clinton is wondering if Andy would paint him. Andy is concerned because Betsy can't stand Clinton. Andy thinks he might get himself into a sticky situation with Betsy. George shows Andy some fake Wyeth artwork for sale on the Internet. He gets thoroughly disgusted.

March 20: Betsy and Andy were talking about me and Betsy said, "You really like her, don't you?" He agreed. She said that I didn't

*like her but he said that I was just afraid of her. I agreed with
him. I would like to be personal friends with her but this would
be impossible with her personality, position and our relationship
with Andy.*

The conversation turned to paintings and Andy indicated he felt some obligation to paint his friend Frolic for an upcoming du Pont show at the Brandywine River Museum. Another possible painting, the one of President Clinton, was troubling Andy. He said he suggested Jamie should be the one to do so. Producer Steven Spielberg wanted to purchase *Night Sleeper* for $8 million but the Wyeths won't sell. If they did, the price would be the highest ever for one of Andy's paintings. Andy asked Helen not to admit she was the model for the nun in *Buttercups* as the owner Leonard Andrews believed it was a real nun.

*March 22: "Night Sleeper" is hanging in his home. He sold the
    painting for $400,000 and later Betsy bought it back for
    $600,000. Now he is being offered $8 million.*

Andy braved a flood to visit the Sipalas. The couple then joined Andy in navigating back roads to view vistas of the Brandywine River from Andy's home. "An awesome view from the back of Andy's home," Helen wrote. She noted that Andy was afraid the flood waters might reach his $8 million painting.

*March 27: Today we discuss James Loper, who lived at the
    Embreeville Hospital and the person Andy painted many years
    ago. My brother Wade remembered him as having played
    baseball and working with my father on the hospital grounds.
    Andy wants to know exactly which tombstone is his in potter's
    field. I researched the question and found all of the records were
    destroyed in a fire. Charles Cawley bought an N. C. Wyeth
    painting from the Sanderson Museum for $250,000. Andy was
    giddish about the episode as that was a lot of money to help keep
    up the Sanderson museum.*
*April 3: Andy gave two prints to the Brandywine Museum to help
    renovate his old homestead. Crawley was disappointed that*

*the upstairs was not finished since he had already given $1
million for that purpose. He pointed a finger at Duff (Executive
Director Jim Duff) and said, "Get busy!"*

*April 5: Andy invited us to see his new painting "Hide and Seek." It
is a tempera of Senna standing nude inside a tree trunk. George
loves it but I personally would rather have seen a child inside
the tree trunk, especially with that title. It's not my favorite as it
is a little too posed. I think he thinks nudes are still shocking but
I disagree but don't dare say anything except praise. Betsy told
him he is ahead of his time, whatever that means.*

*April 8: We had the Wyeths over for a spring dinner party (along
with eight other people). It was unusual evening of local history,
low-keyed people, casual dress and very successful.*

*April 13: Andy appears with Nicky. Nicky is in bad shape. He walks
in tiny baby steps with borrowed crutches from Phyllis Wyeth.
His hips have basically locked. This is definitely a hereditary
gene from Andy. He needs another operation badly but must
take into consideration that he almost died before.*

Andy decided to paint Frolic Weymouth for the du Pont show. The title of
the Senna painting, *Hide and Seek,* was debated. Betsy suggested the title *Dryad*
after the tale of a mystical figure hiding in a forest. The painting won't be part of
the *My Friends* show highlighting Andy's paintings of African Americans. They
are afraid the model might be negatively stereotyped.

*April 22: He showed us the painting of Frolic. It really is quite good.
Betsy sent me a blank book with Christina's World on the front
cover to be used for a diary for the Wyeth dinners. Like it and
will use it.*

*May 8: Today he took me to see the buttercups on Kuerner's hill. He
had me park the car facing our house across the hill. He told
me how much George and I mean to him, how much he enjoys
our visits and how much they lift him. He visits no one else on
a regular basis and hopes to never wear out his welcome. Now,
I realize why he is here. This is his "swan song," just as he has
done every year before going to Maine. He mentions how he was*

in Maine and spoke to his father for the last time. His father said, "Have a safe trip home." That was the last he heard from him. He was notified of his death a day or two later. As he is telling this story, his eyes turn red and tears flow. What he is saying is he might not come back and he wants me to know how much I and we mean to him. It is very sad. He is aware of his age and mortality. This is not a visit that he can share with George.

May 11: Today we talk of how Jamie and N. C. would dream and then paint what they remembered. Andy could never do that. We also talk of ravens and their remarkable appearance and habits.

Helen and George joined Andy and Betsy at a preview of the John McCoy art show at the Brandywine Museum. The Sipalas enjoyed the show and meeting people, including Sally McCoy, Breil McCoy's widow. Sally was a friendly and nice person, Helen recorded.

May 15: Andy mentioned that he can't talk about his father without tearing up. He said at his wedding he was supposed to kiss the bride but turned and hugged his father instead. His father said, "I will miss you down at the studio." They both cried. Betsy was forgotten for the moment.

May 18: Today he surprises us with a signed print of "Jupiter." We seem to be first (or second) of his friends on his mind every day. How fortunate we are!

May 25: The last day we will see Andy until fall. Helga leaves in the morning for Maine.

September 6: He called to say he broke his wrist on his right hand.

September 29: A call. I think he feels more comfortable now that the summer is over and he will be returning home. He is still thinking of us!

October 1: Nicky is doing OK after a 5-hour operation. The Wyeths are relieved.

October 28: He is home but we are at the Chesapeake Bay for the weekend. He left a small tree branch with a note, "A member of

> *your family tree has returned."*
>
> *October 30: Here he is.! I ring a bell upon his entering the yard. Lots of hugs for everyone! George and I see a noticeable change in him: a tired, haggard look. So unusual. His spirits are good. Has old age started to take over? His hearing is getting worse and you have to yell or repeat many things for him.*
>
> *October 31: He surprises us with a Halloween costume. He arrives with his handyman and his (handyman's) girlfriend. He is dressed as a Japanese girl (white facemask and long kimono). We couldn't guess until he walked near a light and I saw his hearing aid. They were on their way to Jamie's annual Halloween party.*

Jamie and Phyllis attended a White House back-tie dinner and gave special guests a signed copy of his latest White House painting. Betsy didn't feel that she and Andy should take away from Jamie's glory day and therefore declined the invitation to attend.

> *December 6: Today he is looking much better and in high spirits.*

On the day of the annual Wyeth Christmas party, Betsy was sick with a cold and can't attend. For several days, Andy and the Sipalas critiqued the party and the guests. Visits and exchanges of Christmas gifts filled the next several weeks.

The year concluded with another disastrous lunch with Andy and Helga. "Why does he do this?" Helen wrote. "He laughs too loud and ignores any advice to lower his voice. George and I are only too glad to get back in the car. These lunches are outrageous and embarrassing! We are always sorry afterwards that we went with them.

CHAPTER THIRTEEN
2001

Andy Suffers a Serious Pneumonia Attack

Andy visited the Sipalas on New Year's Day and continued dropping in on the Sipalas in the early days of January. Helen and Andy discussed his latest painting. Andy mentioned he was using a technique he has never tried before. Only Helen and Helga were aware of his effort but Helen didn't divulge Andy's secret. On another day, Andy told stories about Gene Kelly and President Eisenhower. "Andy is great with stories and can hold you spellbound," Helen wrote.

January 15: This is the day before we go to Washington to see "One Nation." We excitedly tell Andy of our plans. Of course he won't be going.

January 16: It was a good show of Jamie's works.

January 17: Andy wants feedback on the show in Washington. He is thoroughly enjoying it. I thank him profusely for putting us on the guest list. We are most honored and grateful. The "One Nation" show gave Andy a chance to think of great stories of his father and his father's paintings. Andy has such a great memory and is amazed and disappointed when he can't remember a little detail, which happens just a little more frequently.

January 20: Today the conversation includes a lot of American history, which he is fond of.

January 23: Today he talks about his upcoming show in Mississippi ("Close Friends"). He tells us marvelous stories about his black neighbors and friends as a youngster.

January 27: Today's conversation was all about old one-room schoolhouses that are still standing. We also talked about Archie's Church on Ring Road, which now only a graveyard and a stone foundation.

January 30: We talked about N. C.'s illustrations. N. C. mentioned near the end of his life that he was not happy with the work that was offered him. George and I invite Helga and Andy to lunch. Helga is carrying a cellphone in a black leather case with a 6" antenna and wires wrapped around the case. Quite a contraption! She said she needs the extra distance in case something happens to Andy (that nurse image).

February 4: He is very upbeat today because the show in Tennessee went over so well. There was a Dixie jazz band going through the town and at the art show. This show is a genuine display of Andy's friends as a child, teenager and adult. Betsy had wanted to do this show for years but was advised against it.

Andy, George and Helen spent time reading reviews of the Tennessee show and reviewing the show's booklet *Close Friends*. Andy signed a copy for the Sipalas. The trio received some disappointing news about the show that Frank Fowler later reported was untrue. Representatives from Georgia were apprehensive about displaying Andy's show since it included nude paintings.

February 27: He gives me a long letter from a fan. He is turned off by the letter, in part, I believe because of the person's religious reflections. Religion and Andy don't mix, unfortunately. He gives me the letter to keep. Quite frankly, I could understand this writer's feelings but still could see where Andy and this person were not connecting art in the same manner.

March 5: He mentions that Betsy, in conversation, told their niece

*Anna B. how wrong it was for Andy not to tell her about the
Helga paintings. Anna B retorted that she gave him such a hard
time after painting Seri that she didn't blame him. Andy told
Betsy after finishing Seri that if he ever did another nude he
would never tell her. And he doesn't. She had nagged him every
day about which part of her body was he painting. In truth,
and in my opinion, Betsy had certain rights to question him
knowing his character and vulnerability. I'm not sure how I
would have handled it any differently.*

*March 17: George and I were away for the weekend and Andy
used a key to let himself in. We discovered he took the last of
the drawing that were on the third floor. One was a funeral
scene of himself in a casket on Kuerner's hill. He also took the
newspaper clippings that he left with us. I did not realize this
for several days. I was angry with George for not letting me take
the key away from the outdoor hiding place. I was horrified and
disappointed! Not that the drawings belonged to us but the fact
that he planned the move when we weren't home. I felt violated
by this planned intrusion and helpless by George's refusal to take
away the key.*

Helen's anger dissipated as three days later Helen, George and Andy joked
about another one of Andy's early morning excursions into the couple's home.

The conversations among Andy, George and Helen continued as Andy
reported on his experiences with Betsy and the Cawleys. The Wyeths attend
Julie Cawley's surprise birthday party. Helen wrote that she believed the Wyeths
were feeling "a little indebted to Charles Cawley for his airplane services and
donations to the museum. I think they are 'suckered in' completely. It is hard to
turn down such extravagant services and not get personally involved."

If the Wyeths felt somewhat '"suckered in" before a trip to Mississippi,
they would feel even more indebted as Cawley had another lavish trip planned
for the Wyeths.

*March 26: Yesterday Betsy, Andy, Jamie, Ann and the Cawleys flew to
Mississippi to see the show. Cawley had them picked up at their
homes and driven to his airport. Lunch was served on his plane*

and Cawley had men drive his three limos in a large truck to
meet them at the end of their flight in Mississippi. How do you
like that? What money can do! Wyeths, with all their wealth,
were duly impressed by the extravagance. They were all very
pleased with the art show.

Andy and Jamie were selected to receive awards in Washington for being two of America's greatest portraitists. Jamie was designated to receive the award on Andy's behalf. Andy wanted the audio by Morgan Freeman used for his Mississippi show be utilized as an introduction for the Washington vent. "Andy felt that Morgan Freeman could instinctively read his mind and feelings in discussing the paintings," Helen wrote. She added she hoped to get Freeman to join them at a Christmas gathering for the Wyeths.

In the diary, Helen offered additional personal feelings about Betsy.

March 28: Why do I pick on Betsy privately? Because I always leave
Betsy with the feeling that she is in another private world,
opening the door for her benefit and closing it abruptly when
finished. Who can say she isn't polite or courteous but who
can say she is hospitable and warm? Not many, I guess. We
automatically know to keep our visits very brief, never sit down
unless necessary and give her our complete attention.
March 30: He brought us a program for the (Washington art awards
show). Jamie is featured in the booklet with the portrait of
Jack Kennedy and Andy is featured with a side view of Anna
Kuerner. Andy let Mary Landa make the selection. We thought
it extremely amusing, considering the earthiness of Andy's
portrait in such a sophisticated show. George and I thought
it a bad choice, considering so many other of Andy's profound
portraits.
April 2: Today the subject seems to be all about our early sex lives.
It was funny to hear goofy tales from our innocent years. Betsy
saved all of Andy's love letters but burned her letters to him
because they were too personal. As Andy was putting on his
coat, he mentioned he was bothered by ants. We noticed his coat

> *was full of them and we hurried him outside to shake them off*
> *the coat. His pockets were full of food which drew the ants. We*
> *sprayed his car and our kitchen after he left.*
>
> *April 5: He wanted to show us a copy of a letter from Prince Philip of*
> *England. It was a thank you for a gallery book ("Close Friends")*
> *that Frolic sent to him with Andy's note and signature. Frolic*
> *and Prince Philip ware friends and very much into the horse*
> *news.*
>
> *April 13: Andy is painting Jessica Duff nude and he reveals to us*
> *most of the personal information that he gleaned from Jessica. It*
> *just verifies how Andy can't keep a secret!*
>
> *April 19: They Wyeths gave Victoria an Easter basket and she shared*
> *some of her goodies with passengers during a train ride. We all*
> *thought that was generous and cute.*

For the Sipalas, the rest of the spring was filled with social engagements, including a lunch with artist Bill Ewing and his wife, and visits by Andy. Andy was missing from Painter's Folly many days as he was in his studio painting Jessica Duff.

Andy did tell Helen and George that his family was proud that Victoria was accepted at Harvard University for continuing education. Andy and Betsy gave Victoria a million dollar trust fund as a graduation gift and Nicky bought her an apartment. Jamie gave her money to furnish it.

> *May 13: Andy called to have Jessica pose but her parents said she*
> *had work to do that day. He was really disturbed. He was so*
> *disgusted that he wasn't going to call her again. I personally*
> *think the Duffs were concerned for more personal reasons. He*
> *did show George and me the portrait of Jessica and it was quite*
> *lovely. Her parents approved it.*
>
> *May 16: Today Andy, Helga, George and I went to Philadelphia*
> *to see Karl Kuerner's show at David and David. It was fun*
> *walking the streets in Philadelphia.*

Once again Andy used a key to enter the Sipalas home while they were away for a weekend. He spent the time in Painter's Folly clearing out the third floor studio of his notes. A detective wasn't needed to discover Andy was in the house. He didn't close doors properly. Helen wrote she would no longer leave a house key outside Painter's Folly when they were away on trips.

May 21: Jamie received a doctorate degree. We discussed Frolic's health and our concern. There was mention of someone doing a book on Betsy. We all thought it would be noteworthy and interesting.

May 25: Wyeths left for Maine.

The Sipalas made several long distance trips during early summer. First, they attended the opening of Andy's show in South Carolina. Helen reported they were treated royally. Then, in July, they drove to Maine. When the Sipalas arrived, they discovered that morning Andy had been taken to a hospital after suffering a serious pneumonia attack. Andy had to be transported by boat to shore and then by ambulance to the hospital. Nicky was really worried as Andy had a very high fever. Andy told Nicky, "Well, I guess this is it. When's the funeral?"

August 14: He called. Weak but better.

August 30: Andy called about reproductions being sold at Tom Baldwin's Book Barn. Baldwin is reproducing Andy's paintings on canvas by a special machine. Jamie is putting his own attorney on the case. We bought one of "Marriage" and sent to Andy.

October 26: He calls. He is ready to come home.

October 30: He's home! He comes in fine spirits and looks good. I can see for the first time that he has definitely aged a bit.

November 11: We walk along the Brandywine. He uses a cane and walks slowly. He can't walk far, which amazes me. He said his hip was bothering him but I really think his age and recent illness had taken a toll.

November 30: Andy went to Crozer Hospital to have a cataract removed. He really liked his doctor. I remembered the doctor's name and secretly invited him to our upcoming Wyeth Xmas party.

The Wyeth Christmas party took place on December 9 with Dr. Christopher Williams and his wife, the artist William Ewing and his wife, plus Andy and Betsy and family and friends. Later, Betsy personally called Helen to thank her for the fine party.

> *December 14: Andy is doing a portrait of Julie Cawley as a surprise*
>   *for Charles. It truly was lovely. A good likeness of her.*
> *December 20: Andy brought us a special edition of Meryman's 1968*
>   *book on Andrew Wyeth. It has a special blue leather binding*
>   *and gold leaf edge. Andy made a watercolor on the inside page*
>   *of Painter's Folly and signed it. It is just beautiful!*
> *December 26: A wonderful catch-up on Christmas.*

CHAPTER FOURTEEN
2002

Helga Room of Nudes

To begin the year, Andy brought good news about his protégé Karl Kuerner. Leonard Andrews purchased one of Karl's paintings for $140,000. They were all excited for Karl and wished the best for him. Helen wrote a note of congratulations to Karl.

Helen was pleased to receive a call from Betsy concerning jam she make from fruit given to her by Helen. "It seemed so odd to hear Betsy talk so candidly and warm to me and making the call herself," Helen wrote. "I truly was surprised. A rare occasion and one that I will savor." Andy brought jars of Betsy's jam and Helen wrote she believed Betsy's jam was better than the one she made.

January 12: He showed us an article by Joyce Stoner about him in the Winterthur magazine. He was very proud of the story. He told us about a problem involving having Charles Cawley on the board of the Wyeth Endowment. Betsy and Andy wanted him on the board but others believed he was too powerful. Betsy told Andy to handle it. Andy told everyone how it would be: Charles Cawley would be head of the board in Maine. Period! Frolic Weymouth would head the Brandywine location. End of conversation.

January 31: Christopher (Dr. Williams) invites Andy to accept an award at a medical convention. Chris feels Andy was courageous

*and a fine example of an elderly (& famous) person to get a
cataract operation. Andy says he will attend and accept the
award.*

George and Helen spent most of February in Florida. When they returned, Andy said Cawley invited him to Texas to be with President George Bush Sr. for a grand opening of an art show but refused. "Too far," Helen wrote. "Jamie went."

*March 9: Andy said he has trouble swallowing and losing weight. We
are concerned.*

*March 14: Phyllis Wyeth's mother died in Virginia. It was too far
away for Betsy and Andy to attend. Phyllis sent Andy a copy of
the Remembrance program.*

*March 20: Andy's test results were negative. He is pleased. They
"stretched his throat" for whatever help that could make. The
doctor told him to stop all Helga's vitamins, which he will do.
They could be making a residue in his throat. Helga is a little
upset.*

*March 21: We are celebrating the completion of the latest painting of
Helga. Helga had lots of titles that she was looking forward to
Betsy using.*

*March 25: Andy has placed Helga in his will stipulating that she is to
have Eight Bells until her demise.*

*March 29: Betsy named the Helga painting "Gone." He seemed to
think I was jealous of the painting because I didn't rave when I
first saw it. This really was not the case. I was secretly shocked at
how slim he made her. I think I would have preferred a frontal
pose. Actually, the painting was quite good and was typical of
her appearance.*

*April 4: He has been coming later and later over this past year. I don't
think he gets up as early and is slow getting started. His hip has
been bothering him. He hints that he is doing a painting of two
girls naked in a tree.*

*April 5: Someone wants to do a video of him or perhaps a photo
book. The man claims that it will be something unusual and
a different perspective of Andy. He and Betsy agreed to an*

interview, as this man is quite well known. He shows us a recent painting of Irmy. This strange subject fascinates us.

April 8: He reports that he and Betsy have given their approval to the film producer.

Andy was pursuing his request to paint Susie, Helen and George's daughter. Susie was not enthusiastic about the offer. She indicated she believed joking with and entertaining Andy was a nuisance. Susie believed Andy had a dirty mind. According to Helen, Susie thinks Andy has a tendency to ask a person to pose and doesn't pursue the request. "All of this is true but we feel she will regret this after he is gone," Helen noted. "If she made herself more available I know that he would start the painting."

April 10: Helga is not happy with the title "Gone" for her recent portrait. Andy told her the reference refers to love. George gets the dictionary. As he reads, it gets worse and worse and we all start laughing except Helga.

April 12: Betsy named Irmy's picture "Bullet Proof" because of his history and the fact a firecracker blew off part of his fingers. Andy brings us a picture of Helga when she was 19 years old and living in the Black Forest of Germany. She was slim and attractive in black leotards, black flats and black gloves.

April 15: Andy has an appointment with Dr. Bierbaum today to discuss a hip replacement. He is in a lot of pain and is using the cane more than ever. Everyone is afraid of Andy's heart and lungs and his ability to recuperate quickly. (End result: They all opt for pain medicine in lieu of an operation.)

April 22: Some of N. C. and Andy's works are being auction at Sotheby's today from a private collection. Again, Betsy and Andy are very concerned about the prices. He is still doing the painting of the girls in the tree. He is being very secretive about the subject matter and likes to tease us.

May 6: He is disturbed today. He found out that Lee Conklin has an art shop filled with too many signed prints in Chadds Ford. Jamie (and others, I suppose) have insisted that he stop signing any more for this particular man. He is really disgusted today.

> *We can't blame him, even though this man has been collecting*
> *and selling for over 30 years. Andy is concerned about an*
> *upcoming trip to New York. Will he be well enough?*
> *May 14: Charles Cawley is concerned about who will replace Frolic*
> *at the museum if Frolic dies. This is a concern for the Wyeth*
> *Foundation.*

Cawley flies Andy to New York in his private plane for the award presentation at Wheaten College. He gave an amusing speech, Helen reported. Andy was upbeat as the Sotheby auction prices for his paintings were high.

> *May 28: Andy would like to attend Leonard Andrew's opening of*
> *his private museum but will be leaving with Betsy for Maine*
> *before the opening. Charles Cawley is flying them to Maine in*
> *his private jet. He offers me a gift of money for "putting up with*
> *him so much and serving him food but I protest. I tell him that*
> *I will not be paid for the joy of seeing him and enjoying his*
> *company and laughter. It literally brought tears to my eyes with*
> *that horrible connection but I was touched by his thoughtfulness*
> *and generosity.*
> *May 30: He didn't visit but left with Betsy for Maine.*

In July, Helen wrote a long letter to Andy and Betsy about the events around Chadds Ford and wished Andy a happy birthday. Most of the summer passed without contact with Andy.

> *October 29: HE'S HOME! He looks good and is full of stories.*
> *Betsy is furious with Ann Cole for selling a painting to Charles*
> *Cawley that Andy gave her. Betsy tells Ann that she was going to*
> *put her on the board at Farnsworth but now won't do that.*
> *November 4: I told him that I am redecorating a bedroom and will*
> *be placing all Helga nudes on the walls. He is excited. He starts*
> *thinking of what he can donate in line of an ORIGINAL. He*
> *said Helga would be pleased. I ask him to sign some nude prints*
> *and he said, "I'll sign anything you want." He knows we never*
> *give away or sell anything he gives us.*

Andy accepted a Doctor of Fine Arts degree from Wills Eye Hospital in Philadelphia but he kept the award secret. Jamie had just received an academic award and Andy didn't want to detract from his son's accomplishment.

Helen and George accompanied Andy and Helga to the Philadelphia Art Museum. Once again Helen noted that Helga's behavior was an embarrassment. Helga touched Andy's paintings, claiming ownership and took photographs when told not to do so.

November 10: Andy shows us a painting of Betsy in Charles Cawley's airplane called "Heavens to Betsy." It is very good and very interesting!

November 11: Today is the big day that we show Andy the two redecorated bedrooms. The nude pictures are hung. He is shocked and very pleased and excited with our end results. He is really excited and mentions that Helga would love to see it when complete. Next we surprise him with his former studio across the hall. This is truly a shocker. This is truly his favorite. I told him that I was placing all Chester County landscapes in there because there is a good view on the Battlefield from the window. He goes to the window and stares out. What was in his mind will be a mystery for a while. I'm glad he is excited and not disappointed that we cleaned up his room.

November 19: He revealed that he has a special account for Helga that is near a million so she will be taken care of when he dies. Betsy changed the name of her painting in the airplane to "Above it All."

November 22: He seems to have more time to visit. Could it be his age?

Andy counseled Karl Kuerner on the business of the art world when Karl received a low return of money from a sale at an art dealer in Philadelphia. Andy compared Karl's problem with one he faced as a young painter. "People are out to take advantage of you while you are young and need the money. It is a sad scenario," Helen recorded Andy as stating.

Preparations took place for the upcoming Wyeth Christmas party, including selecting guests.

December 12: Betsy has renamed the latest painting "Plane Chair" and I'm not thrilled with it or its meaning. The other name was better.

December 14: Xmas party! We sent a private car for the Bierbaums at the airport. Four clarinets and a bassoon were played by students from Avon Grove High School.

December 16: Andy couldn't visit Sunday because he had to take the Bierbaums to the airport, so he came today. He just raved about the party. Betsy said it is the most unique party each year.

December 21: Andy and Helga bring us Xmas presents of "Helga on her Knees" and "Widow's Walk" for the 3rd floor, just as promised.

The year ends with a visit to the Chadds Ford Tavern for lunch with Andy, Helga and Jessica Duff. They returned to Painter's Folly where Helga and Jessica viewed the Helga prints. Andy stayed downstairs and fell asleep on the couch.

CHAPTER FIFTEEN
2003

She Keeps Me Alive

The first week of January was devoted to entertaining a patron of the Brandywine River Museum at Painter's Folly and discussing needed repairs to the home. The ceiling in the family room was cracking and Andy suggested calling a noted architect to inspect the damage.

January 9: He hints of painting Jessica Duff in the back of his car. Evidently, a nude painting is in the making. He said "the model" was complaining about the car exhaust as it was making her sleepy. Betsy has changed the airplane again to "Otherworld." Will this be the last change? He said Frolic is preparing a dinner party for the opening of Jamie's art show "Capturing Nureyev."

January 16: Anna B sold the Santa Claus painting to Jamie for $1.1 million. Frolic wanted to buy it but the price as too high. Anna B needed the money as her husband was going to school and money was tight. N. C. gave it to Ann McCoy who in turn gave to Anna B. Usually, Andy frowns on those who sell his work thinking they only want the money and can't appreciate the art. Not so in this case.

January 19: Betsy is very concerned about the expected biopsy of the sore on her face. It worries Andy too.

January 21: We pick up Andy and Helga and have lunch at Bill and Mary Ewing's house. I swear, Ewing's paintings are unbelievable and pure in detail, color and arrangement. There surely must be a place in history for this man's art. What a God given talent! I couldn't help but wonder how Andy felt when looking at Ewing's work. Andy has a lot of respect for Ewing and always did recommend him for portraits.

The Sipalas spent some weeks in Florida during February. During an exchange at Valentine's Day, Andy sent them a note and sketch of him in a long winter coat painting in the snow. Helen wrote, "We are thrilled! A priceless gem!" The house keys were removed so Andy couldn't gain entrance while they were away.

Upon their return, the Sipalas took fruit to Betsy. Betsy's surgery was successful.

March 29: Andy calls us to go out for lunch and preview his new painting. The painting was of Allan Messersmith. It was called "Home." Allan stood in the snow and Andy sat in his open heated van while painting. (We laughed about the unfairness of it all.) It truly is one of my favorites.

April 9: Andy gave us a signed print of "Pentecost." He said he knows we don't care for it. George mentioned that it wasn't his favorite. Wrong thing to say! Though said innocently, Andy was slightly offended. Andy said he envisioned the nets in Pentecost looking like spider webs. He was fascinated with the contrasting colors. It is on the island now called Allan Island. A girl drowned there years ago and Andy envisioned her blond hair flowing through the water, a feeling connected with the flowing nets.

April 23: Andy asked George to buy him a lightweight lawn chair for sitting while painting. George picked up two for him.

April 29: "I'm sorry, I've come with bad news today," said Andy. Louise Kuerner (Karl J. Kuerner's wife) has breast cancer and had a mastectomy three days ago. Karl said privately that the

doctors are afraid they might not have gotten all of it. Andy is
very sad about the situation. Andy asked that nothing be said to
others. She was out working in the garden, so I see her as being
strong and tough in her fight with cancer.

May 1: MAY DAY! Thoughtful and touching! While I was out of my
kitchen he placed this basket along with a very small figurine
of four Dutch girls dancing in a circle. The whole thing was so
delicate! I will keep it forever and he knows that.

In early May, Andy received hospital treatment for his throat. He was
concerned with the choking that occurs when he eats. He had lost weight. Helen
wrote, "It also bothers him at nighttime and he finds that sipping on vodka by
his nightstand will soothe this throat and let him sleep. We are all puzzled by his
problem." During the same conversation, Andy expressed concern for Frolic's
health.

May 12: Andy received a good health report but is concerned about
losing weight. He is now 140 lbs. and can fit in old clothes!
The "Architectural Digest" is on the market (with an article on
Betsy). He was honored that the article was about her instead of
him. Andy and Betsy attended a wedding at Frolic's chapel and
the relatives ignored Betsy. Andy feels it was jealousy about the
article. He was very defensive today and felt that Betsy didn't
deserve the snub.

May 13: I've never seen him so offended by the relatives and so
supportive of Betsy.

May 19: The Chinese are doing a film on Andy and should arrive this
week. It will probably open that market for him.

May 22: The Chinese are in town and Mary Landa is showing them
around.

May 23: Andy was quoted in Richard Meryman's book, "The Secret
Life," that he abhors being fussed over and pampered because
he had so much of it while young and in frail health. Isn't it
ironic that Andy is now in that very same situation with Andy
getting old and Helga playing the nurse? "She keeps me alive,"
he frequently says.

*May 25: Any day he will be leaving for Maine. He drives over the
hill and behind the Kuerner homestead. We talk about the
buttercups and how each of us must remember their meaning
when one of us departs. "I will always be there, floating around.
Just remember that," he says very softly. He tenderly gives me a
kiss while holding my hand and then slowly leaves the Kuerner
property.*

*June 29: Gone! It takes me about two weeks to unwind and get him
out of my system. It is both relief and sadness. Goodbye my
friend.*

As Helen did the previous year, she wrote a long letter to Andy and
Betsy during the summer about happenings in Chadds Ford. Andy and Helen
exchanged telephone calls and additional letters in August about events in Maine
and Pennsylvania. Andy wasn't the only one reading Helen's letters. Andy told
Helen that Betsy enjoys her letters.

*November 4: Here he is again! He needs a haircut and looks
weathered. I see more aging. Little does he know that we are
preparing to put our house on the market in the spring.*

*November 20: We read the letter from Odd Nerdrum accepting our
invitation to our Xmas party and then read the letter declining.
Andy was amazed that we made contact with him and was
disappointed that he can't come.*

December 5: First snow of the season (5 inches) and in blows Andy!

*December 9: Andy calls us to the Mill to see a new painting,
"Portage." It is a painting of a water scene near his home in
Maine. The water is of such different moods that Betsy thought
it should be called "A Self-Portrait." He revealed how he was
sitting so long painting that when he tried to get up he couldn't.
He reached for a branch, it broke and he fell into the water.*

The Wyeths' Christmas party took place on December 13. As usual,
guests were suggested and rejected for the party. Some of the guests came late
and some canceled because of illness. The party was deemed a success by Helen
with the usual top-notch food and entertainment.

December 22: Victoria and Andy surprise us with a visit early in the morning. Susie joins us for tea. We all go to Hank's for breakfast. Victoria is completely off the wall. She shocks all of us but admits to doing this for "shock purposes." I really like Victoria and have watched her grow up. How she will turn out is a wild guess. She is attractive, personable, intelligent and an important part of the Wyeth dynasty.

December 24: Andy tells us that he and Betsy have put Victoria on the Wyeth Foundation's Board of Directors. Victoria is delighted.

December 29: Andy asked Allan Messersmith to pose nude. He refused. Andy offered $1,000. Allan said he wouldn't do it for $10,000. Andy asked why. He said it would be beneath his dignity. Andy is shocked, disappointed, but impressed with his honest answer. Andy is looking for a dark eccentric person to pose nude with Indian feathers. A new and different idea for him. David McCallis (who is writing a book about Betsy) asked Betsy why Andy never painted her nude when he asked so many others. Betsy said, "I don't know how to answer that. I don't know." With that, she asked Andy. Andy said she didn't like to pose. "I can imagine and fantasize about others, whereas I enjoy all the love and romance with Betsy. There is a difference," Andy said. Andy indicated that there was a moment of awkwardness for everyone with the question.

CHAPTER SIXTEEN
2004

Betsy Was Right for Andy and His Work

The good and bad news in January was that *Widow's Walk* sold for $2.5 million, a figure that Helen believed Andy may be exaggerating. The Sipalas were sad to see the painting depart but were happy for Andy and Betsy. The painting was one of the earliest Wyeth's paintings hung in Painter's Folly.

Note: It is now 3/24/04 and I haven't written anything since the last day of December 03. I now have to rely on George's notes and my memory. Too bad!

March 15: Today he talks about being retired. I ask how he is doing with one of his paintings and he said he is retired. "It is just that I don't want people to expect much of me."

March 18: He brought us a copy of "American Artist Magazine" that had an article about his art techniques. He was very pleased with the article.

March 24: He gets a coughing spell and couldn't stop. After some real concern I offered some Vodka. He eagerly took it and the coughing stopped. He said it was the tightening in his throat. He said it is also stress. I found that statement unusual because

*I really never connected stress with him. When I hugged him I
noticed that his shoulders are mostly bones with little muscle.
With those heavy wool sweaters it is not noticeable. This really
surprised me.*

Helen spent April Fool's Day with Andy and noted she forgot to "fool"
Andy. She assisted with selecting a frame for a pencil drawing of the Mill and
flood debris surrounding a large tree. Andy will give it to Betsy as an Easter gift.
It is quite effective.

*April 6: Today is pick-up time for the finished painting. He talks
about meeting Betsy for the first time and how he proposed to
her on their first date. She accepted. We laughed about how
bold he was and still is. She was right for me and my work, said
Andy. She stood behind me all the way and believed in me even
though she was only 17 and I was 21. He is relaxed and eager to
share stories with us.*

*April 13: I tell Andy about our plans to move. George just can't
handle the place anymore. More importantly, he just doesn't
want to. "Will you move to Florida?" he asks. After questions
and answers, he said, "Go ahead and sell the place!" I told him
that George might not like it because I told him. Andy proceeded
to write George a note: "George: Sell the place and take your
time and get a good price. Good luck, Andy." "This means that I
can't visit you anymore except maybe once a year," he said."*

*April 19: We talk again about the sale of our house. I don't know
what his feelings are but I would guess sadness, resentment,
disappointment, a lost feeling and probably many other
emotions. How sad for all of us.*

*April 24: Kuerners invited us to join them at a pig roast at the farm
for museum benefactors. Andy didn't want to go but Helga told
him the Sipalas will be there and he agreed to attend. He took
us on a tour of the house where people trailed along behind us
and cameras were flashing. Very soon he had enough and left
abruptly with Helga scrambling to fix food platters for Helga,
Andy and Messersmith.*

> *April 26: Andy brought the finished Messersmith painting to show us.*
> *He painted the crown of thorns on Messersmith and was looking*
> *for our opinions. It truly is a great painting, which I considered*
> *neither Jesus Christ nor even religious. A very deep and moving*
> *painting that evoked many thoughts that I tried to express.*
> *Andy was listening intently and appreciated very word. We all*
> *wondered what Betsy will name it.*
>
> *April 28: Today he is excited to tell us Betsy's reaction to the painting.*
> *First she named it "Mourning Mae." She was very moved*
> *by it. After a day of looking at it she started with criticism.*
> *"Have you gone soft on me?" she asked. She took the painting*
> *as too religious. She thought the Sipalas put him up to it.*
> *When family, workers, Frolic and museum associates said it*
> *caused such profound reactions (weeping and many serious*
> *conversations) that Betsy started taking a second look and*
> *offering a different opinion. Somehow, religion does not sit well*
> *with her. How sad! Frolic said he would buy it immediately. She*
> *declined. She'll show it in the museum next month.*
>
> *April 30: Betsy has renamed it "Crown of Thorns." Phyllis told her to*
> *not show it for about a year because it is too close to the movie*
> *Passion and people will associated the painting with the movie.*
> *We agree with that premise.*

Andy confided that he is having another disagreement with Betsy over Helga. Betsy accused Andy of giving away studies to Helga and threatened to visit the studio to look for the sketches.

Before departing for Maine, Andy again asked to paint Helen's daughter Susan. This time Andy does sketches of her.

Andy's mood lightens as he prepares to depart Chadds Ford as he reported his paintings were fetching high prices at auctions.

> *May 24: He is a little more open about saying goodbye. I'm sure he is*
> *more concerned than ever about his health and his demise. We*
> *hug and wish him well and he responds a little sadly. He will be*
> *leaving tomorrow morning.*
>
> *July 7: He called to say that he saw our house for sale. He said, "I*

hope it doesn't sell until I'm dead." We try to reassure him that
we will still be around for a long time.

October 19: Another call. We haven't heard from him for a while. He
is excited and said he will be home soon.

October 29: He's home. He looks tired and a little weak. I doubt if he
will climb our stairs again. It is just too difficult. He had fallen
in Maine and hurt his ribs; plus his hip is hurting again. He
still has a wonderful smile and likes to tease but we do think he
has to force it more now.

November 3: Andy has come up with a guest for our Christmas party.
His name is David Moses Bridges from Maine. Andy has been
painting him. He is a native Indian and makes birch canoes.
Andy said he is making one for Betsy for Xmas (a surprise).

November 9: Andy brings David Moses over to meet us. We tour the
downstairs and then walk over to the battlefield to look at the
trees. David is young, married, has a son, and long, black, wavy
hair.

November 23: I attended Victoria's tour at the museum (she began
working at the Brandywine River Museum). I was so impressed
that I told Andy about it. He suggested that I write to Betsy with
my opinions. I do that.

The annual Christmas party was held on December 11. Andy, Betsy
and nine other guests attend. Betsy looked tired and older that night, Helen
recorded. Betsy's appearance was unusual as Betsy was usually vibrant in public,
according to Helen.

December 22: Helga and Andy came for lunch. The lentil soup made
Andy cough profusely. Bad choice. He has been having trouble
swallowing. He showed us a Howard Pyle painting that Betsy
gave him as an early present. It was an original illustration and
just beautiful! Betsy won the auction bid from Sotheby's. Phyllis
Wyeth was trying to win the bid but Betsy told her to forget it
because she was determined to get it.

December 29: He showed us a personalized book that Sen. John
Kerry sent him. I guess Kerry thought that Andy had supported

him in the campaign for President but it really was Jamie.
Andy is a devout Republican and thought it a howl that Kerry
sent him the book. He and Betsy both detest him because Kerry
ignored Betsy years ago when introduced. No forgiveness on
their part!

New Year's Eve found Helen and George with Helga and the Kuerners at a Chadds Ford home. Everyone found an "instrument" for music. Lots of food and a great time, according to Helen.

CHAPTER SEVENTEEN
2005

God Help Our Wonderful Friend

Andy was in great shape mentally and physically during one of his first visits of the year to Helen. He enjoyed a hearty snack before discussing his latest painting.

> *January 5: He is painting Allan Messersmith in the woods,*
> *hanging on a cross and almost naked. He is trying to convince*
> *Messersmith to disrobe completely. I have some real reservations*
> *about Andy depicting Messersmith as Jesus. Has he gone too*
> *far? There was a lot of emotion about the crown of thorns in his*
> *last picture of Messersmith. How will people feel about it? How*
> *will Betsy react? If he does it nude, I will really be bothered by*
> *it, especially since Andy is an atheist. We talk about our many*
> *Xmas guests over the years and suggests I write a book about it.*
> *Is he testing me?*

Andy and Helen talked about the artist Peter Hurd, who married Henrietta Wyeth. "He said Peter Hurd taught him a lot about art, martial arts, the military, protocol and sex. "Anything I say or do is because I love you, not to hurt you," Andy said Hurd told him. Andy said Hurd played the guitar, sang and was a great artist (better than John McCoy), handsome, intelligent and a very good friend.

*January 7: He brings a letter from a convict sent to him from
prison. The prisoner wanted Andy to send him some originals
and signed prints. It was the most pathetic letter. Andy and
Edward Hopper each have a painting of significance hanging
in the Philadelphia Museum of Art in a special area. A real
compliment! Andy is really proud.*

*January 12: Andy said that "Distant Thunder" sold for 12 million
to Bill Gates. Gates would like to meet Andy. Mrs. Woolworth
bought a painting for $65,000.*

*February 1: Andy told us about being invited to the White House
for dinner on Valentine's Day. Betsy said no. Andy said, "They
must think we're still 16 years old. We're too old for that kind of
travel." President Bush would like to buy Andy's painting that is
hanging in the White House.*

*February 6: Andy and Betsy won't be going to the White House for
the dinner party but instead are doing something "more exciting
for them." Andy won't tell us but evidently it is a response to the
invitation by the Bush family.*

*February 14: Andy showed George a letter from President Bush
thanking the Wyeths for the donation of the "Jupiter" painting.
Andy was very excited. How interesting this is, considering the
Wyeths' stature. Both Betsy and Andy were thrilled to show the
correspondence.*

Betsy announced at a dinner at the Dilworthtown Inn that David Hastings
would replace her on her personal trust board after she is deceased. Her board
had been nagging her to find a replacement.

*February 24: He isn't feeling well today. He is distressed with his
tiredness. Losing his appetite.*

*March 16: The painting "Jupiter" was given to the White House.
President George Bush Sr. wrote Betsy and Andy a personal
letter of thanks. Andy was really proud of this, just as I would be
about something of Andy's.*

*March 29: Spain is having one of his art shows this coming year.
Andy is thrilled. It will be a "first" for him. Spain got the idea*

from seeing "Jupiter" hanging in the White House. The same
show will be in Philadelphia later on. Betsy is sending most of
her private collection to this show.

April 4: Andy is still feeling tired. He needs energy to work and drive
but doesn't have any. He looks as tired as he feels. That lively
spirit has faded.

April 11: He drags himself in today, feeling all washed out. He had
a mole taken off his face near his eye. The doctor is getting a
special shot for him to boost his energy.

April 14: He caught us in bed this morning. I felt bad that he had to
climb all those steps in his weakened condition. He is anxious
to tell us that there is nothing wrong with him. He just has low
sugar. He is so relieved and happy. "I'm not going to die after
all," he laughs. "You'll have to put up with me a little longer."
He gave us a print of "Man in Dory" and signed it.

April 20: He still lacks energy. Peter Coggins, his plastic surgeon,
wanted to do some face work on him but Andy said, "Like hell
you will!" He is still losing weight and is down to 131 pounds.
This concerns him. Doesn't have much of an appetite.

Andy's health continued to decline. He contracted pneumonia and was very sick. He had prostate issues and an infection in his lungs, liver and kidneys. He continued to lose weight and was getting weaker. "Still he manages to smile and pretend things are not as bad as he feels," Helen wrote. "We manage to laugh and joke and Andy said, 'At least we can laugh about it.'" Later, Helen wrote, "God help our wonderful friend."

Andy's health didn't improve during his annual summer trip to Maine. Helen noted three times in a short telephone conversation he said, "I'm on my way out."

July 18: He called thanking us for his birthday gifts. Victoria must
have gotten after him about the "on my way out" business. He
tried to sound good but he is not himself. Still not painting.

Victoria called Helen after visiting Andy in Maine. Victoria reported Andy was painting again and regaining some strength. She was encouraged after seeing her grandfather. Victoria's call eased the concern felt by Helen and George felt about Andy.

Andy returned to Chadds Ford in October and looks "much better" than when he departed, Helen wrote.

> *October 30: He joins us wearing a handsome leather outfit similar to*
> *Robin Hood. Someone ordered it for him and he actually looked*
> *handsome in it as it was so "his type." He looked very much the*
> *(Robin Hood) part. We rave about it and take pictures.*

Helen and George flew to Atlanta to attend an opening of a show of Andy's works at the High Museum of Art. Museum officials gave a formal dinner and were excited the Sipalas attended, according to Helen. "It is always a 'big thing' for the models to attend an opening," Helen wrote. "We were pampered and lots of photos were taken. Such a strange thing to be 'famous' for a day. It is hard for me to receive this attention but at the same time we both know what a privilege it is to be part of Andy. He made us what we are and without it we are nothing!"

> *November 10: Ann Wyeth McCoy dies.*
> *November 14: Andy talks about the death of his sister, Ann McCoy,*
> *and to invite us to her memorial service. Andy is calm about her*
> *death but realizes that he is the last surviving Wyeth from N. C.*
> *Wyeth.*

The Sipalas attended the memorial service for Andy's sister. Andy said he went to the funeral home and painted Ann. Andy asked his nephew to take some pictures of her but the nephew was aghast at the idea. Helen recorded, "Why not? Andy said to us that (his) father said to do this and spend time with the dead as that is when you really connect with them."

> *November 28: He said he added sled marks on the painting of*
> *deceased Ann, called "The Last Ride."*
> *December 10: OUR XMAS PARTY FOR THE WYETHS. The*
> *dinner went smoothly. I told George later that this might be*
> *the last party for them. It is a lot of work, money and time and*

leaves out entertaining our personal friends. If we cannot find new, exciting people for the Wyeths, it isn't worth it! It must be planned months ahead to get the right people. If not, we end up with the same locals.

December 23: He tells us about an interview he had with the "New Yorker" magazine. When the question arose about the Helga paintings and would he do it again, Betsy told Andy to lie on the floor, which he obediently did, and she stood over him with a knife indicating what would happen if he did something like that again. She challenged the writer to take a picture and print that! This article comes out in January or February '06. How dangerous can you get? Andy is painting Betsy's hands while she is knitting. This should be interesting. He "kicked Karl Kuerner's ass" for not painting his bedridden mother. Karl is now reconsidering the idea before it is too late. He and Betsy received a letter from President Carter applauding the Wyeths for the wonderful show in Atlanta. He and Betsy were extremely proud and delighted.

December 27: Today he arrives with a new coat from Betsy. It is copied from some knight or king era. He left it on during the whole visit. He told us he now weighs 123 pounds and Betsy is not happy. They don't understand the weight loss. The first news of the morning was that Nicky got married three months ago and just announced it to the family. When Victoria heard the news while visiting Nicky, she bolted from the door and left for Chadds Ford. She was very upset. The rest of the Wyeth family is happy with the new wife and welcomed her.

CHAPTER EIGHTEEN
2006

Like Making Love in Public

Andy and George enjoyed a New Year's Day tea while Helen attended church. Andy was sporting a new coat given to him by Helga. Before departing for three weeks in Florida, Helen and George spent a number of days having lunch with Andy and Helga. Lunches were the main outings for the Sipalas and Andy during the first part of the year.

February 13: He sounded awful. Two days (since) throat surgery by
> *Dr. Coggins.*
February 14: He looked awful and I felt sorry for him trying to
> *eat, even though I made potato soup for him. He has lost more*
> *weight and was not recovering quickly from the surgery. He had*
> *a cyst on this throat that had been bothering him for about a*
> *year. He is wearing a neck brace while the stitches are in.*
February 24: He enters and George is seated at the table with a mask
> *on and a newspaper in front of his face. We all get a good laugh*
> *out of it. He looks good and the stitches are out of his neck. Yes,*
> *he does look better and maybe a little younger.*

Andy invited Helen and George to an opening of his show at the Philadelphia Museum of Art. The day before the opening Andy toured the show with Betsy and he became dizzy. The museum staff gave Andy a wheelchair but he soon discarded the chair and continued the tour on his own. "We believe he was overcome by anxiety on seeing his own works," Helen wrote. "He truly is terrified of showing and seeing his works in big shows. 'It is like making love in public,' laments Andy. 'Suppose the show doesn't go over?'"

The Wyeths approved of the Philadelphia show and the publicity generated. The show was the first time the Philadelphia Museum of Art acknowledged Andy. Helen wrote the lack of recognition "has annoyed Andy for many years. It is with disgust and rage that he knows that he has been so slighted for so long. Isn't it amazing that suddenly 'they' fall in love with him? That museum always favored European work and contemporary artists."

March 28: There was a big article in the "Philadelphia Inquirer" rehashing the show. There was a quote from George and me. The paper was kind to Andy this time, which surprised Andy. He always expects the worst.

March 29: There was a TV program on Wyeth and the Philadelphia show. There was a close up of our home (Painter's Folly) and "Marriage." Andy is proud indeed.

April 14: Andy brings a painting that he bought for Betsy from Karl Kuerner. He asks George to go to the Mill with him to carry it in the house. It is a large painting.

April 15: Andy and Betsy invited George and me to see Karl Kuerner's new picture. Betsy tells us to close our eyes until seated. We are staring at a large watercolor of frogs walking on lily pads with umbrellas. We all just love the painting! Betsy said she is crazy about it and very excited. We all agree it is the best and most unusual painting by Karl.

April 19: He comes in with a copy of the "New York Times." He said, "I told you they would take a swipe at me." It is an unkind article just as he predicted. He said Betsy enjoyed our visit. Betsy said, "No wonder you like the Sipalas. They're 'real' people." Jamie and Frolic weren't as excited about the frog painting.

May 4: He walks in with Tom Hoving's newest book, "Wyeth on Helga." He is concerned that Betsy will have a fit. He asks us to read it and tell him honestly how damaging it might be. I can say that it is a passionate love story and one that is sure to

*rile Betsy. George thinks it is the same old information with the
exception of Andy saying he destroyed some artwork of Helga
because it would ruin his marriage.*

*May 6: He comes back to hear our opinion of Hoving's book. I
thought the book was a passionate love story. I said Helga would
be proud but Betsy will chew him out big time. We hear the
book will be sold at the museum. Insiders are trying to stop it.
Andy says he can't show too much anger because it will only
make the book more credible. We agree. Nicky said "the hell
with it," it's the stuff that's been written about before. Most
people don't think it was nice of Hoving to write it now.*

*May 13: He finished a new painting called "Catfish," and then it was
changed to "Up Stream."*

*May 15: We tell him a "Philadelphia Inquirer" reporter is coming to
interview us about the widow's walk. He thinks it is a good idea.
My goodness, he looks awful today!*

*May 17: He asks George to get him the June edition of "Smithsonian"
with an article about him. He said it is the best article that has
been written and we are excited to read it. He said he and Betsy
are to fly to Maine on Charles Crawley's plane on May 26.*

Betsy and Andy departed for Maine as scheduled but returned a few days
later after Betsy was told she needed surgery as a lump in her nose was malig-
nant. While recovering, Betsy tripped and cut herself, necessitating stitches in
her leg. Helen wrote, "Andy is concerned about Betsy and realizes he can't leave
her alone, ever. 'She is fragile,' said Andy." Betsy and Andy returned to Maine
in early June.

Andy called George and Helen twice from Maine. Helen wrote Andy a
long letter on August 3. Helen inquired about Betsy's health and asked if Andy
was behaving himself. She then related some local and family news.

*November 5: He's back! He is looking really good. We tell him about
our visit to New York to see the Helga collection at Alderson's
gallery.*

During the show, Helga drew a crowd. Everyone was given a Helga catalogue and a chocolate candy with a picture of Helga. Helen met Larry and Klara Silverstein and Larry revealed he was the owner of Twin Towers 6, destroyed in the terrorist attack on September 11, 2001. "I about dropped my teeth and goose bumps ran down my arms," Helen wrote. Silverstein told Helen he was to go to the doctors that day but his wife dissuaded him. His children also escaped death on 9-11. Silverstein then accepted Helen's invitation to attend the Wyeth Christmas dinner on December 2.

> *November 8: He told us that Elizabeth Campbell (Campbell's Soup*
> *Company family member) bought a 6 million dollar picture of*
> *his.*
> *November 14: Andy told us Frank Fowler brought Elizabeth*
> *Campbell to our home with her two children. We were away.*
> *She took photos of the outside of our home since she owns*
> *"Widow's Walk." Too bad we missed her.*

The Christmas party was held and Silverstein and his wife attended. Betsy was sick and Victoria was upset she was not invited. "A very interesting group of people," Helen wrote. Three string musicians from the Darlington School of Art performed.

> *December 4: Andy comes to rehash the party. "The best ever!" he*
> *exclaims.*
> *December 13: He is doing a painting of Mrs. Kuerner in bed. He*
> *told Karl that if he didn't paint her, he would. Karl said he just*
> *couldn't do that painting.*
> *December 16: We have a party for our own friends, including*
> *Victoria. Victoria is still bent out of shape for not attending the*
> *"Wyeth" dinner. She stays for a short time. Victoria will not be*
> *invited to our private parties again.*

CHAPTER NINETEEN
2007

A Presidential Tour of the White House

Andy was sick and didn't visit during the first few days of January. As with the past year, many of the outings with Andy revolved around lunches.

Note: 10/26/07: I'm just now recording my diary from our notes. I have a lot to cover and will probably abbreviate our visits. It's hard to get into this sometimes when I'm busy with other things.

January 4: He looked good and was in good spirits. He doesn't like to discuss any illness.

February 22: He came for tea after our being in Florida for several weeks.

March 6: We rejoice to see Andy again.

March 20: We discuss the upcoming film on Chris Sanderson. Andy has great feelings for Chris and fills us in on stories of the past.

April 4: Andy invites us to see his painting of Betsy. It is of Betsy's hand knitting. Great idea and wonderful painting.

May 12: Andy is doing a Quaker painting of his new housekeeper. He comes to us to get help in finding a Quaker bonnet.

> *May 26: Andy has a new print of "Snow Hill" for us. Can you*
> *beat that! Nicky visits because Andy is being operated on next*
> *Tuesday. His throat is giving him trouble. He is not looking*
> *good and very weak.*
> *May 30: Andy is in the hospital. His trip to Maine will be delayed*
> *this year.*
> *June 3: Here he is again! Right out of the hospital and to our*
> *breakfast table! He is still very weak and looks terrible but is*
> *trying to keep his spirits up.*
> *June 11: This is Andy's last visit before going to Maine. Andy just has*
> *not been well. He lost a lot of weight and is weak.*

Helen sent two letters to Andy while he was in Maine but received no responses. Late in October, Andy sent Helen and George a letter. Andy felt guilty about not calling or writing but Helen didn't expect him to do either because of his age and health issues.

> *October 30: He's back! He brought us up to date on the sale of his*
> *paintings. He looks good and we are all glad to be together*
> *again.*
> *November 4: He is excited to tell us that President Bush has invited*
> *the Wyeths to an achievement award dinner. We rejoice with*
> *him. He is so humbly proud.*
> *November 9: Betsy will be going with him to Washington for the*
> *award dinner on November 15.*
> *November 17: Andy is anxious to tell us about the trip to*
> *Washington. President Bush took Andy and Betsy on a private*
> *tour of his living quarters and showed them where Andy's*
> *painting was hanging. After the trip, Betsy and Andy couldn't*
> *sleep with all the excitement.*

The annual Christmas party was held on December 8 and Betsy had a great time. Helen wrote, "Betsy was in a rare mood, brought on by the antics of Dick Taylor. 'I've never had such a good time in my life,' she laughed."

> *December 13: Rehashed our party. He was especially pleased that*

Betsy had a good time. He said he is doing a large tempera and is excited about it.

December 26: We pick up Andy and Helga for a surprise ride. We take them to St. Cornelius Church for a private Christmas tour with MSGR. Parlenta. We totally surprise them.

CHAPTER TWENTY
2008

I Love You

Andy was missing the first few days of January. He called to say that he was fine but he still didn't visit.

January 16: He came and found us in bed. He loved it! The little
rascal!
February 17: We're back from Florida and he has come to catch up on
the news.
March 7: Andy invites us to the Mill to see his newest painting,
"Goose Step." Truly, it is a fine painting, so natural with the
Brandywine and a strutting goose. I just love it.
March 17: I fix St. Patrick's lunch for Andy, Helga and Tommy
Drane. We all wear silly green hats and lots of green clothing.
April 3: He came to tell us about his doctor's tests which were
invasive. Having a hard time swallowing. Feeling a little better
but not happy about it.
May 7: Another visit with news about the sale of one of his paintings.
May 9: We had lunch with Andy and Helga at a restaurant. Andy
told us about an observer who offered to buy his painting for
$24. Little did the stranger know about the artist at work.

Before departing for Maine, Helen and George teamed with Peter Coggins for a surprise trip for Andy. Coggins dressed in Amish clothes and waited alongside a road. When Andy and friends stopped to help a "sick Amish man," Andy didn't recognize his doctor. Andy introduced himself as a "painter."

Coggins said he painted also and asked Andy if he would like to see his barn. Andy finally commented that Coggins looked familiar and the doctor then pulled off his wig. "We all howled with laughter," Helen wrote. "It was a perfect success. Andy had been had, real good!"

November 1: Andy's back. He really looks bad. He lifted some heavy chairs in Maine and he thinks he broke some ribs when he tripped and they fell on him. He is ashen colored and is hurting.
November 6: Dolly stops in and said Andy is sick and down for the count. How sad to hear.
November 11: I took Amish soup and food to the Wyeths' house. Betsy greeted me while Andy was upstairs in bed. Helga is with Andy 24/7. She sleeps on a mattress on the floor beside Andy's bed while Betsy sleeps in the guestroom.

The annual Wyeths' Christmas party took place on December 6 without the Wyeths. Kevin Pierce, a retired state policemen, sang and entertained. "How wonderful!" Helen wrote. "When everyone arrived I suggested we all jump in cars and sing outside Andy's house while wearing Santa hats and ringing bells. We sang "Jingle Bells" and "We Wish You a Merry Christmas." Helga and Victoria helped Andy out of a chair and he came to the door with an oxygen tube in his nose. How pathetic and sad. We were all devastated but Andy seemed delighted that we came."

December 15: I came home to find Andy, Helga, Denny & Carolyn McCoy (Ann Wyeth's son and wife) in the house enjoying our Christmas trees. It is the first time we have seen Andy since November 1. I am just overcome with joy, sadness and elation. Andy is walking but Helga must assist him. All I could say was 'I love you' over and over and that we missed him. So bittersweet to see him.
December 25: Christmas Day at 11 a.m. Helga drove up blowing the horn. We ran outside to see Andy sitting in the car with the oxygen hose still in his nose but smiling broadly. Andy wanted to see our Christmas trees once again! He was so happy to be here and we were shocked that he made such an effort to see us. Again, all I could say was "I love you."

CHAPTER TWENTY-ONE
2009

May God Bless Andy Wherever He Is

Helga called George and asked for a favor.

January 3: Helga said Leonard Andrews died and would we get a copy of the "Philadelphia Inquirer" to take to the studio. We did. We found Andy in bed dressed in a nightshirt and sports jacket. He was glad to see us. Such a strange scene: All of Andy's paintings props and elements hanging on the walls, sitting on the windowsills or plopped on the floor. No carpets but two beds, lots of medical equipment. A mist vaporizer was running in the corner and every chair was loaded with items typical of Helga. This is where Andy wanted to be, free from company and Betsy at the Mill. This was also freedom for Betsy as she can't stand being around ill people, even her own husband, especially when Helga must be with Andy 24/7 as his nurse. Andy tries to be valiant by raising his fist and saying, "I'm going to get up and around soon." When will we see him for the last time? He might surprise us.

The January 3 visit proved to be the last visit by Helen and George to their dear friend, Andy Wyeth. Victoria called Helen and George at 4:40 a.m. on January 16 with news that Andy had died.

> *January 16: The family had him discharged from the hospital yesterday with hospice care and they placed him in the Long House (across from the Mill.) Victoria, Helga and the hospice nurse slept there with Andy. The hospice nurse woke Victoria that he was passing away. She held his hand and talked to him. They talked about the painting "Snow Hill," which is in fact the 'dance of death.' She told him that she would call all of his friends and then told him it was all right to go. With that he died. She then woke Helga and called Jamie and Nicky. Jamie and Helga proceeded to paint the death scene, which is exactly what Andy would have done.*
> *Victoria went to the Mill and turned on the light in Betsy's bedroom and told her that he died. Betsy sat up in bed and screamed fiercely. She said he would be buried in Maine in Christine Olson's family cemetery. It will be private.*

Less than five hours after notifying Helen and George of Andy's passing, Victoria and attorney Bill Pricket arrived at Painter's Folly to see if Andy had left any paintings or money. Helen wrote, "We are in shock that this would happen only hours after his death. Perhaps this is the proper thing to do but we were still in shock with Andy's passing. They apologized. They made several more of these stops, elsewhere."

> *January 18: Helga and Victoria stopped in for tea. Helga is distraught that she is being forced out of Andy's studio. Victoria is trying to calm her by promising that she would do all she could, with the help of Jamie, to keep her there. She insists that she needs a place to paint and write poetry. Victoria is getting frustrated and wants to leave. George questions Victoria about the funeral on Monday but Victoria cuts him off because Helga is not to know, as she is not invited. Victoria mentions maybe it is Wednesday, again, fooling Helga.*

*January 19: George and I take our own family out to dinner as a
closure to Andy's death. It is a round table and we gave Andy
a toast "to yesterday, today and tomorrow." Then we all held
hands and said a silent prayer for him. We exchanged some
stories about Andy and felt like we truly said goodbye to him in
a small way.*

*January 23: There is a pre-arranged preview party at the museum to
honor Caroline, Andy's sister. Since it is so close to Andy's death,
the crowd is huge. We think the public is looking for a way to get
closure on his death.*

A call from Joyce Stoner revealed some information about Betsy and
Andy's final moments. During the call, Stoner asked if Helga could live in the
carriage house on the Sipalas' property. That request was denied.

*January 29: She said Betsy is angry with Victoria and taking her
grief out on her. Betsy is feeling left out not being with Andy
when he died. Even when Andy was home for the day (from the
hospital and in hospice care) and within walking distance from
Betsy she refused to see him and thought she might visit the next
day, which was too late. She truly has a phobia with hospitals
and death.*

*January 31: The Brandywine River Museum has a two-day tribute
for Andy. Before 9:30 a.m. the line of people is far out in the
parking lot and about 4 deep. (Displayed) is a huge photo of
Andy with university capes hung on either side (very colorful).
Below the picture is a plastic case holding all his medals. As the
line circles you come to a glass enclosure with Andy's French
uniform on a mannequin.
Inside the gallery is a painting of "Christina's World" that was
loaned by the New York Metropolitan Museum of Art. Also there
is the last painting of Andy's called "Goodbye." Downstairs in
the lobby is another large photo of Andy on the wall surrounded
by a garden setting. Black drapes hung from the second story.
Very impressive and sad but definitely giving closure to his
death.*

Frolic Weymouth held a luncheon for "special people" associated with Andy on January 31. Helen and George attended. Helen wrote, "Andy would have loved it. We saw so many of our 'surprise guests' from years past who attended Andy's Christmas parties at our home."

January 31: We were invited to dinner with two of Andy's doctors: Mitch Kaminski and Joe Valotti. The Kaminskis were the hosts. Joe was depressed about Andy and we were to try to lift him in some way. All were looking for closure.

MAY GOD BLESS ANDY WHEREVER HE IS.

POSTSCRIPT

Correspondence

Helen and George received a number of letters after Andy's death. The following are several of them.

Dear Mr. and Mrs. Sipala,

My deepest sympathies on having lost a dear and talented friend. I thought of you immediately when I heard that Andy Wyeth had died, and my heart went out to both of you. You had a rare and unusual friendship with one of the most well-known artists in the world, one who immortalized both of you, and yet, for all the glamour and celebrity, I know that what is missing the most is someone who was close and cherished.

I've heard from Linda that you knew each other for 23 years, almost a quarter of a century. I still remember your story about noticing someone sneaking about the property, and rather than finding some thug or vandal, you discovered an artist – who was very familiar with your home – and then discovered a good friend.

I also remember you taking me to hear his granddaughter talk about him and his paintings; what a delightful afternoon that was. I had just seen the Wyeth exhibit in Philadelphia, had seen your cases in "marriage" and was now listening to the voice of the granddaughter reveal myths and truths about the very man that had become such an unusual part of your lives. I still have the calendar that Linda gave me featuring you for November. What a wonderful gift.

I'm sorry for all of us that Andy is gone. I always thought if God was fair, he would take the worthless, the stupid and the mean and let the earth grow under the voices and batons and paintbrushes of the bright and talented. I remember crying when Fred Astaire died. We miss the ones who sing and dance and paint, who bring joy and color and light … and who knew light better than a Wyeth.

And what a good friend you were to him, too. I understand that it was not easy to get into that inner circle, and that his wife protected him fiercely, so surely the Wyeths felt just as fortunate to have met loving and genuine people. Maybe that's the real story here; not that you knew the Wyeths, but that they knew you.

I hope friends and family have been a support to you. I didn't call or write right away because … well because the grief is so deep, you just can't read another letter or card, and the words just float into the air and get lost with all the other words. I just thought if I have this a bit of time, you might know how much I've thought of you since that day, and how I will never ever think of Andrew Wyeth without thinking of the name Sipala right next to it.

Good thoughts, good health. Be well, be kind.

—Karen Jessee
(Educator and writer)

August 6, 2009
Mr. and Mrs. George E. Sipala
Dear Helen and George,

Here's a note that come out of the blue! Obviously I was distraught when I learned of Andrew Wyeth's death. I'm finally collected enough to send you a few lines. I only met him a few times but he was such a memorable presence that those moments with him are etched vividly in my memory, and it was always nice to look forward to the notion that I might get a chance to meet him again. I would have little conversations in my head imaging that possibility.

His passing makes me all the more grateful for the dinner party you hosted which made it possible to see him a last time. And getting to know you added a new dimension to what I knew about his personality - gave me a new appreciation of his vitality, his sense of humor, and his courage. And of course it's quite a thrill to look at his paintings of Painter's Folly and to think that I slept in one of the upstairs bedrooms. You clearly meant a lot to him — it was exciting to meet you and meant so much to see him one last time, even in failing health.

With all best wishes,

—Henry Adams
(Art historian, professor and museum curator)

Dear Helen and George,

On the way home from work, I heard the news of Andy's death.

The memories I have of Andrew Wyeth are of a man with a breadth of wonder and a healthy sense of humor. The memories themselves are a precious gift. Thank you for making opportunities.

Hope you are well and enjoying memory sharing.

My love,

—Sr. Loretta
(Order of the Daughters of Charity)

February 4, 2009

I had such a wonderful time in Chadds Ford with the two of you. It helped heal the grief of losing Andy just to be there … and to be there with you. You treated me to great meals and great conversation and remembrances.

I can't thank you enough for the opportunity to look through your scrapbooks. I have never felt more rarely privileged. It is such an intimate portrait of a friendship, through the passing of time. I am so very, very glad that you took those pictures and saved those notes and doodles. Thanks also for the pencil and brush, which I am having framed for safe keeping. I will treasure them forever.

I never would have had the friendship with Andy that I've enjoyed these past nine years, apart from you. Andy and I connected forty years ago, when I was barely nineteen, but we became real friends because of you. When I met you guys in 2000, I instantly <u>liked</u> you both – immensely so. I felt at ease around you, and, by my second or third visit, I felt you were family. I told Andy so, several times.

I honestly think the two of you were the closest friends he ever had in Chadds Ford. He and Frolic go back fifty some years, but Frolic's was never a "drop in" place. There was always a certain formality about their relationship. He hasn't had a friend in Maine since Walt Anderson died in 1984. Whenever I would be in Maine, he always asked when was the last time I've heard from the Sipalas. I think you're stuck with me as well.

See you soon!

—Dave Hastings
(North Carolina art collector)

Editor-In-Chief
Bruce E. Mowday

Bruce E. Mowday is an award-winning author and newspaper reporter. He has authored more than books on history, sports, business and true crime. Mowday has appeared on the *Discovery ID* channel, *ReelZ network, C-SPAN,* the *Pennsylvania Cable Network, Hollywood and Beyond,* Whatcha Got, *Journey into the Civil War, Chronicles of the American Civil War* and television shows. He is a frequent speaker at various civic and historical groups. The Congress of Civil War Round Tables has named Bruce a "5-Star" speaker. Mowday has hosted his own radio shows, has been editor of magazines. For more information on Mowday, his books and his schedule of event*s, see www. mowday.com.*

Over the years Mowday read a number of books on Andrew Wyeth, N. C. Wyeth, Jamie Wyeth and the rest of the Wyeth clan. He spent many hours at the Brandywine River Museum of Art looking at the wonderful collection of Wyeth art in Chadds Ford, Pennsylvania. The Wyeth paintings became like old and treasured friends. Mowday authored the book *Stealing Wyeth,* about the theft of 15 paintings from the Andrew and Betsy Wyeth estate. He covered the case as a newspaper reporter.